TAP
DANCING
THROUGH
LIFE

Published by Advantage, Charleston, South Carolina.
Member of Advantage Media Group.

ADVANTAGE is a registered trademark and the
Advantage colophon is a trademark of Advantage Media Group, Inc.

Printed in the United States of America

ISBN: 978-1-59932-049-6
LCCN: 2007935964

TAP DANCING
THROUGH
LIFE

7 STEPS to **FINDING YOUR PERSONAL RHYTHM** and **ACHIEVING THE LIFE OF YOUR DREAMS**

VAL GOKENBACH

DEDICATION

To Rick, Rick and Nikki
All my love forever!

CONTENTS

ACKNOWLEDGEMENTS

I would like to acknowledge the following individuals who have helped make this dream of writing a book come true for me.

My husband Rick, for his endless faith in me and his personal tolerance of all the strange and wonderful things I have tried and accomplished and not accomplished throughout our life together. I love you!

My wonderful kids, Rick and Nikki who have inspired me to provide for them a role model of success and determination. Their personal strength and determination through their life challenges with diabetes give me an ever-constant source of pride and belief in personal strength. I am so proud of you guys.

My mom, who has taught me independence and strength, and has instilled the life values that have continually guided my life. Mom you taught me well.

Elizabeth Jeffries, a wonderful mentor and coach who began me on this journey to fulfill one of my lifelong dreams to write a book and take a wonderful step to helping others through this opportunity.

Ann McIndoo, my writing coach and now friend who is an amazing individual and who has inspired me and instilled in me a self confidence for writing that I never new was possible. Thank you Ann for being you.

INTRODUCTION

Welcome and thank you so much for joining me on this tremendous and exciting journey to personal exploration and achievement. It is my belief that learning about yourself and loving yourself are your first steps to being yourself. You have made the first step to embracing yourself and recreating your life.

This book utilizes the fun metaphor of tap-dancing to describe the vast variety of rhythms in the universe that affect our lives. You will learn how these rhythms impact facets of your life such as health, thinking, and your future. Several exercises take you through analysis of your present life situation, followed by processes to develop personal goals and objectives to achieve your desires. Rhythm success factors are included throughout the book to help you stay on course. You may even pick up some tap steps along the way!

In this book, I will be your personal life coach and confidant through this journey so feel free to write anything you like as you evaluate your present life and chart your goals for a more successful you! It is not as hard as you think; you can do this!!

CHAPTER I:
WHAT ARE RHYTHMS?

OBJECTIVES: CHAPTER 1

1. To understand what are rhythms. To know there are rhythms in the universe, the body, and in our human behavior.

2. To learn what are your own personal rhythms.

Why Tap Dancing?

I love to tap dance so I chose tap dancing as the metaphor to teach you about rhythms, as you will see, *tap dancing is all about rhythm.*

I started dancing when I was three years old and had every intention of becoming a professional dancer; it was my life's goal while I was growing up. However, performing is not steady, predictable work so I was concerned about how to afford to live between performing jobs. As a child, I was taught the value of money and the need to work and support myself. A very dear friend of mine, who was a nurse, suggested that I study nursing. She said that the nursing profession would allow me to have a flexible working schedule and to be able to get a job in any hospital. I decided to pursue nursing with every intention of spending most of my time on stage.

Well, that's not exactly what happened. Following my graduation from nursing school, I discovered I really loved nursing! I found it very rewarding to help people and make a significant difference in their lives, however, I could not forget about my love for dancing and decided that I had to figure out a way to be able to keep dancing in my life. I opened a studio, started local dance companies, and performed whenever I could. Through this approach, I found that I could balance my love for dancing and nursing and feel very fulfilled and happy with my life. I especially enjoyed the rhythm of movement and the effect it had on my body.

I will be combining several concepts to help you learn about your rhythms to create balance in your lives. I will help you look into personal situations and find ways to improve the quality of your rhythms to achieve your desired success. Life is just like the rhythm of tap dancing. Think of this the next time you watch a dancer, some moves are slow, some are fast, some are complex, some are melancholy, and some are up beat and happy, just like life. We all have good days and bad days. Sometimes our rhythms are slow; sometimes they are upbeat and fast, some are chaotic, and some are slow. The goal is to understand these rhythms and harness the ability to balance and manage them. Just like tap dancing!

What Is a Rhythm?

Let's first define the term rhythm. The dictionary describes rhythm as a strong, regular, repeated pattern of movement or sound. These repeated patterns are all around us. If you concentrate on your current environment you will be able to identify several rhythms. Perhaps you hear the regular drip of a faucet or the sounds of your air conditioner or furnace (depending where you live) switch on and off. These are rhythms. Maybe you are focusing on your heartbeat or your breathing patterns; these are also rhythms in your life.

If you are outdoors, you may realize that it may be dusk or raining which represent rhythms in weather and our day and night cycles. Maybe it's time to take your dog out for a walk. Pets have personal rhythms just like we do. So, as you can see, rhythms are everywhere.

Circadian Rhythms

The major rhythms that we are most concerned with as human beings are what are called Circadian rhythms. These rhythms are directly associated with changes that take place over the course of a twenty-four hour day. You wake up in the morning when it becomes light, you get tired in the afternoon after lunch, and you become very tired in the evening when it is dark and time to sleep. Our bodies are on this twenty-four hour cycle clock, or Circadian rhythm.

In fact, the word Circadian derives from the Latin *circa*, meaning around, and *diem*, which means, the day. So, these rhythms are based on our twenty- four-hour clock. These clocks drive our behaviors and the phenomenon of rhythms in our lives and universe. If we learn to understand them, we can use them to our advantage. So, let's start talking about some types of rhythms and how they affect our lives.

Rhythms in the Universe

We live in an amazing world synchronized by forces and energy that have come together to create the world we live in. Imbedded in the world are those rhythms we identified earlier. We will now discuss rhythms that are familiar to you.

Seasons

One of the rhythms we have learned to be comfortable with is the changing seasons. Seasons change with the cycles of the sun, which alter the environment we recognize as different seasons: Spring, summer, fall, and winter. Reflect for a moment on your favorite season. What you probably notice is that you pick the season where you feel that you are your best. There are those of us who like the activities in warm weather and are comfortable with the heat. There are people that feel comfortable in the cold and those who like the colors and scenery of fall. Some of you enjoy the renewal of the world during springtime. Personally, I love warm weather and feel better when I have a longer day. For me, the longer days provide me with more energy and the feeling that I am more alive. Regardless, these preferences become a part of your personal rhythm. You choose activities around them, vacations around them, and perhaps have changes in your health around them. One thing we know for sure is the fact that we need to learn these rhythms, adapt to them, and live with them. Take a moment at this time to identify which season is your favorite and why. Also think about the ways you adjust your life to accommodate the seasons that are not your favorite.

Rhythms in Nature

Other rhythms in the universe that you may be familiar with are also linked to changes in seasons. For instance, what happens to the trees? They lose their leaves, and the flowers become dormant. Even in areas of minimal climate changes plants and trees are in a constant stage of change and renewal. These are all rhythms.

Weather

There are also rhythms in weather. Rainy seasons, hurricane seasons, and snowstorms are all components of repeatable patterns of weather. Even if there is variability in daily weather, overall rhythms are very predictable.

For those of you who travel and frequently find yourself in an airplane, you may have noticed how much turbulence there is during summer versus winter months. This difference has to do with the rhythm of the weather and what happens to air stability. Air is more stable in the winter resulting in less turbulence whereby heat and storms during the warmer months may result in more bumps when you fly.

Animals

Animals provide a great study in rhythm. Bird migration is an example of a fascinating rhythm in the animal kingdom. How do fish know when and where to spawn? What about the types of animals you see in the daytime versus animals that you see at night? Even animals have a day and night shift. Hibernation patterns of bears and other animals are also predictable rhythms.

Take time to observe your pets. What rhythms do you recognize in their behavior? Is your dog waiting for you when you come home? Does your cat follow you to be fed? All of these are rhythms. Life in the animal kingdom is also about rhythms.

Rhythms in the Body

Physiological rhythms are vital to our health and quality of life. The term "physiological rhythm" refers to what happens to the physical body, which is affected by our twenty-four hour clock. This concept is the most important in this book and will be the focus of the next chapter. To be successful, we need to learn how to evaluate and control our personal rhythms.

Rhythms in Human Behavior

What about human behavior? Our Circadian rhythms affect our human behavior as well. When it gets dark, we sleep. When the weather changes, we dress appropriately in order to adapt to that change. Human beings are actually very good at adapting to change even though we often resist it. We are also creatures of habit. Which is why we feel the most comfortable where we're in control of our personal rhythms.

I'll give you an example. What happens when you sleep through your alarm clock and wake up late? Your rhythm is off. You feel stressed. Or, when your kids are sick, there goes your rhythm. There goes your family's rhythm. There goes your kid's rhythm. These events also throw off your predictable work rhythms. You are now out of control and forced to adapt your rhythm to a pattern that is outside your comfort zone.

There is even evidence that our physical movement and vocal patterns are predictable rhythms that change for different circumstances. Rhythms in learning behaviors have also been identified in students. Students learn better during the morning hours. If you are interested in someone, or angry with someone, your vocal patterns change to accommodate the message you are trying to communicate.

Even little variations in our rhythms can have serious affects on our lives and stress levels. Imagine the pressure secondary to serious illness or injury. I will tell you a little bit about what happened to me seven years ago. I was the victim of a mountain biking accident. To me, mountain biking was a challenge as well as a way to be able to commune with nature. To keep in shape and maintain my level of training, I would regularly ride for several miles early in the morning. While riding this particular morning, a large dog came out of nowhere and ran in front of my bike. I hit the dog head on and the clips of my shoes did not disengage. I was thrown head over heels with my bike landing on my left side shattering my left wrist and arm. I was scheduled to travel to Florida with my family to teach at a fitness convention later that afternoon. This was to also be a vacation for the family. Needless to say, the kids and my husband were very disappointed with this unexpected turn of events. I was rushed to the emergency department with my hand in terrible shape. After the physical exam I told the physician that I needed to be on a plane by two o'clock that afternoon. His comment to me was, "The only place you're going to be at two o'clock is the operating room." There went my predictable rhythms for quite some time. I ended up in the operating room only to emerge with a titanium external fixator for twelve weeks followed by a year of physical therapy. Talk about throwing off my personal rhythms. I found that without the use of my left arm, as well as the bulk of the external fixator, I could not perform the simplest of tasks. I was very much out of control and forced to craft a whole new set of personal rhythms.

Take a moment to reflect on times in your life where you felt that you were really out of control. How did it make you feel? What did you do to get workable rhythms back in your life?

Learning About Your Personal Rhythms

We live our life in a very busy world. We are stressed, we are moving, we are constantly caught up in the chaos and don't have much time to reflect on ourselves. This constant activity can lead to rhythms of behavior that may be out of balance and detrimental to our well-being. Part of this chaos has to do with the roles that we play in our lives and the stress inherent in those roles. You may be a parent, an employee, a husband or wife, or a friend. These roles place different pressures on you and contribute to the establishment of your personal rhythms. The first step in our journey of self-exploration is to identify the personal roles that we play.

For me, I was a child, daughter, girlfriend, fiancée, and dancer. I became a nurse. I am a public speaker and hospital administrator. I am also a mother and wife. Over time, these roles have provided varying degrees of pressure resulting in changes in my personal rhythms.

To help you identify your roles and personal rhythms, you will be doing two exercises in this chapter. The first is an exercise in role identity, and the second is charting your personal rhythms.

Directions Role Identity Exercise

Take a few minutes to think about the roles you have played in your life up to now as well as the roles you are currently playing. Feel free to go back as far as you like. Using the Role Identity Tool, write down all that you can remember. Take a moment to think about the roles and everything you have accomplished in your life while in that role. Evaluate the roles and identify how they helped to establish your personal rhythms, which ones were more difficult than others and which ones have you enjoyed the most?

CHAPTER 1 EXERCISE: ROLE IDENTITY LIST

1	
2	
3	
4	
5	
6	
7	
8	
9	
10	
11	
12	
13	
14	
15	
16	
17	
18	
19	
20	

RHYTHM IDENTIFICATION TOOL

The next exercise will prove very insightful for you. In fact, the first time I did this it was frightening to see the rhythms that emerged in my own life. I was visually able to see tremendous imbalances that affected my health and my perception of my life. Please make the commitment to completing this exercise since this will take you a week to chart your activity. It is important to observe your rhythms over time since one day will not give you a trend. Have fun with this.

Directions

Begin by looking at the grid. There are several specific rhythms that we will be discussing throughout this book that contribute to your overall health such as sleeping, eating, exercising, and renewal activities. We also need to identify your work rhythms and other ways you spend your precious time.

Begin by looking at the left column, which represents hours in the day from 12 AM to 11PM. Simply put a dot in the box that coincides with the activity for the categories listed above. For instance, if I were going to sleep at 10 PM, I would put a dot in 10 PM, 11 PM, 12 AM, etc., until I got up in the morning. The next day, once again chart your hours of sleep and so on. Repeat this for all of your activities. You should end up with a dot in every hour of the day. If you do something on the half hour, chart it in the box closest to the hour. For instance, if I eat at 12:30 in the afternoon, log it in the 1pm box. Chart your exercise hours and any renewal activities that you engage in such as relaxing, reading, watching TV, or other hobbies.

The last section deals with work schedules and "other." When you chart your work hours, it is important to include the time spent commuting back and fourth to work or hours spent completing work at home. Use the other category to log tasks that are necessary but are a drain on your time such as shopping, laundry, driving kids, or doctor appointments. Chart your activities for a whole week.

When you are finished review your grid, reflect on your patterns and identify those that you think need to change. When I did this, I visually saw the numbers of hours that I was working and realized I needed to make some changes to provide more personal time. That effort always seems to yield limited success for me, but at least I made an effort and have an awareness of the rhythm. This chart is designed to give you some insight into your personal rhythms so that you have an idea of where you could begin to make personal improvements. We will refer to this chart through the remainder of this book.

IDENTIFY YOUR PERSONAL RHYTHMS

(see tables on pages 23-25)

	Sleep							Eating							Exercise							Renewal Activities							Work/Other							(Explain)
	M	T	W	T	F	S	S	M	T	W	T	F	S	S	M	T	W	T	F	S	S	M	T	W	T	F	S	S	M	T	W	T	F	S	S	
12a																																				
1a																																				
2a																																				
3a																																				
4a																																				
5a																																				
6a																																				
7a																																				
8a																																				
9a																																				
10a																																				
11a																																				
12p																																				
1p																																				
2p																																				
3p																																				
4p																																				
5p																																				
6p																																				
7p																																				
8p																																				
9p																																				
10p																																				
11p																																				

	Sleep							Eating							Exercise							Renewal Activities							Work/Other							(Explain)
	M	T	W	T	F	S	S	M	T	W	T	F	S	S	M	T	W	T	F	S	S	M	T	W	T	F	S	S	M	T	W	T	F	S	S	
12a																																				
1a																																				
2a																																				
3a																																				
4a																																				
5a																																				
6a																																				
7a																																				
8a																																				
9a																																				
10a																																				
11a																																				
12p																																				
1p																																				
2p																																				
3p																																				
4p																																				
5p																																				
6p																																				
7p																																				
8p																																				
9p																																				
10p																																				
11p																																				

	Sleep							Eating							Exercise							Renewal Activities							Work/Other							(Explain)
	M	T	W	T	F	S	S	M	T	W	T	F	S	S	M	T	W	T	F	S	S	M	T	W	T	F	S	S	M	T	W	T	F	S	S	
12a																																				
1a																																				
2a																																				
3a																																				
4a																																				
5a																																				
6a																																				
7a																																				
8a																																				
9a																																				
10a																																				
11a																																				
12p																																				
1p																																				
2p																																				
3p																																				
4p																																				
5p																																				
6p																																				
7p																																				
8p																																				
9p																																				
10p																																				
11p																																				

Next Steps

Here are your next steps. The point of this chapter is to show you the existence of rhythms all around us and to get you to begin to understand how rhythms affect our lives. Hopefully, you now realize how rhythms affected the choices you have made in the past and how they may affect the choices you make in the future.

It is only through self-discovery that we learn to make better choices and understand why we make the choices we do. This personal knowledge is what will help guide successful decisions to help make the most of our lives.

TAP DANCE INSTRUCTION: TOE DROP

I told you all that this was about tap dancing. So, just for fun I included a tap step to coincide with each chapter. Here is your first step called the toe drop. Stand on one leg and dig the heel of the other foot into the floor. Follow this by dropping the toe to the floor creating two sounds. Repeat this on the opposite leg. Find your rhythm and perform this as fast or as slow as you like. You have learned your first tap step.

CHAPTER 2:
RHYTHMS IN YOUR HEALTH

OBJECTIVES: CHAPTER 2

1. Learn about the importance of personal rhythms and their relationship to your health.

2. Learn the components of good health.

3. Learn about the importance of rhythms in prevention of disease.

4. Have an opportunity to evaluate your present health.

Rhythms & Health

Health has been simply defined as the absence of disease, but it is far more than that. Health is a holistic combination of all that we are as human beings including our physical, mental, and spiritual conditions that work harmoniously to create balance. If you are not balanced in one of these components, then you are not experiencing total health. People can be suffering from physical disease, experiencing mental problems, or be lost spiritually. Any one of these conditions can result in misalignment of the total being.

Look back at a time in your life when one of these components was not in balance and see how it affected you. One example in my life was the day that my mom found a lump in her neck. Our worst fears were realized when it was diagnosed as cancer requiring a radical neck dissection followed by six weeks of daily radiation therapy. At eighty-three years old, we were concerned about the great deal of stress this would place on her. She is a very strong person and did very well with her treatment; however, we noticed that the entire series of events also placed mental and physical stress on the entire family. We worried about mom, but we also needed to adjust our lives to help her recover from the initial surgery, get her to treatments every day, and periodic doctor appointments. In the background were the continual fears of reoccurrence, complications, and potentially the loss of our mom.

I consider myself pretty healthy, but through this stressful time found myself repeatedly ill. I had frequent colds, continued flu-like symptoms, chronic fatigue, and inability to sleep. My brother and sisters seemed to have the same experiences in their own lives. Once my mom was doing better, it was like magic. I became better. My family became better. Our rhythms returned to normal.

Common Rhythms in Health

There are many observable rhythms in our bodies that are necessary to our health. The following is a list of several that you may or may not have realized.

- Stress hormones peak in the morning resulting in an increased blood pressure.

- Most heart attacks and strokes happen in the morning because of the increased stress hormones.

- Growth hormones are secreted when we sleep.

- Cholesterol levels peak in the evening.

- Jet lag is caused by the disruption of our internal clock, especially across time zones.

- Seasonal affect disorder (S.A.D.) is directly related to decreased exposure to sunlight.

- Your body temperature drops at night.

- Your body temperature increases with activity throughout the day.

- Working night shifts can affect your health if the lighting does not replicate daylight and if you don't sleep in total darkness during the day.

- Your organs are affected by your personal rhythms.

- Your nervous system and your reaction time slow down when you are tired or when your rhythms change.

- Your coordination is best around 2:30 PM.

- Your greatest cardiovascular efficiency and muscle strength peaks around 5 PM.

- Bowel activity is suppressed around 10:30 pm.

- Your joints are stiffest in the morning.

- You are more creative in the morning.

- Most moms go into labor in the evening hours.

- Reproduction and fertility can change with changes in your personal rhythms.

- Monthly menstrual cycles are rhythms.

Components of Health: Physical Condition

It is important to realize that there are various components that contribute to our total health; the first is our physical condition. How do you feel physically? This is generally what we think of when we think of being healthy. If we feel well, we assume that we are healthy, but that is not the entire story.

Through lifestyle practices and personal choices, many of us live in the state of pre-disease that we may not realize. Practices such as smoking, drug use, excessive drinking, and poor dietary habits contribute to the state of pre-disease. These behaviors start us on the road to disease in the future. The good news is that we have control over these choices.

Here is an example. Have you heard about hypertension? Almost everyone has. How many of your friends or family members have hypertension? Unfortunately, probably several. Do you have hypertension? Hypertension is prevalent in our society and is a lifestyle disease that begins because of the choices we make in our personal rhythms. We don't include the necessary healthy rhythms in our lives. These rhythms include exercise, healthy eating habits, decreasing stress, and getting enough rest. The problem with hypertension is that it is just the beginning of a whole host of diseases that are much more serious than hypertension itself.

For instance, kidney disease starts because of hypertension. Cardiovascular disease and heart attacks can be a result of hypertension. Type-II diabetes, which is reaching epidemic proportions in the country, can begin with hypertension. Changes in our personal rhythms and, mind you, small changes in our personal rhythms can move you from the pre-disease state into a state of health.

Lessons From the Nurse

I've learned several lessons as a nurse that have helped guide me through personal choices that have altered my own rhythm. I will share them with you as food for thought.

> *First of all, people who become sick always regret that they have not taken better care of themselves.*

When we are healthy, we take our lives for granted. We could be in a state of pre-disease and not realize what our rhythm choices will cause in the future. What is important to remember about pre-disease is that it takes a long time for diseases to manifest signs and symptoms and by the time we experience these physical changes, there is usually significant and oftentimes irreversible changes in our health. We are lulled into believing we're okay even if we are in a state of pre-disease.

Regardless of how wealthy and powerful you are,
you are not immune to disease.

I have experienced working with many wealthy, powerful and seemingly important people over the course of many years nursing. We are all the same when we are ill. Illness and death are great equalizers.

You only have your health. Without good health you cannot enjoy all
that you have worked for over the years of effort.

You probably have heard stories of individuals who have worked themselves to death for personal goals and money. Maybe they have sacrificed their families. Maybe they have sacrificed relationships. Regardless, if you are sick or dead, you cannot enjoy the life you have dreamed of.

The body is amazing and forgiving.
The body has the power to heal if we give it the proper care.

We will be spending time on this concept in later chapters. Your body gives you second chances if you take the opportunity.

Lastly, we only have one life. You can't buy it with money.
All you can do is the best job possible to take care of yourself.

Components of Health: Psychological Condition

The next component of health is the psychological condition, or what is going on in our minds. The effects of our own mental thought processes on the human body have been receiving increased interest over the years.

This is an amazing science. Many physicians are calling the study of our minds the next frontier as vast as the study of oceans and space. Scientists have said that we have not begun to unlock, investigate, or understand the power of the human mind. Research has now found evidence that our mental processes can change both the quality and the status of our physical state for either the good or the bad.

A physician by the name Leonard Hayflick did studies on stress in 1961, particularly what happens to cells in the body during stress. It was observed that, under stressful conditions, the aging process accelerated. The cells become old leading to an early death. They also lose their ability to divide and reduced their immunity to invading organism. These findings have serious implications to our health considering the body's need to renew cells in order to live, but it's also important because most of us live in a state of constant stress. Our body replaces itself over a period of time due to a phenomenal renewal process. We need to allow our bodies to recover and to carry on with this vital function.

Dr. Candice Pert also discovered neuro-peptides that communicate with the immune system and the mind. She termed neuro-peptides molecules of emotion, which affect changes in the energy of the cells in the body. She observed that these molecules of emotion were responsible for several changes in the cell, which included a decrease in the immune response (decrease resistance to disease), increased secretion of adrenaline (which kept the cells in a state of stress) and an increase in blood pressure leading to clogged arteries, depression, fatigue, and insomnia. If we go back to the story I told you earlier about the situation with my mom, the physical changes experienced by myself and my family were probably due to the high degree of stress. It decreased the ability of the cells to renew and maintain resistance to invading organisms and led to frequent illnesses. This suggests that we may have some control over our illness if we can harness control over our mind. Remember, you are what you think.

A whole new area of study is emerging that is incredibly exciting called 'psycho-neuro immunology.' This science studies the mind/body connection and its relationship to disease. Very fascinating! We will be discussing these topics later on in the book, so you'll learn to apply some of these concepts a little later.

Components of Health: Spiritual Condition

The last component of health is that of the spiritual condition. I am not defining the spirit in the context of religion so I am not making any suggestions to whether you should be religious or not. That is your personal choice. This just attests to the fact that we all have some type of spiritual belief system that guides our life.

The notion of spirit in this context is defined as something that transcends the physical world and us. I am religious so for me, my spiritual condition is grounded in my faith. You may believe in God or the universe or nature, all of which are greater than us. A spiritual focus in our lives provides hope and meaning to whatever we do. It has been found that people who are spiritual, regardless of their personal religion or belief system, handle adversity, disease challenges, and stress more successfully than those individuals that have no spiritual belief system.

Balance

To be healthy, however, the rhythms of all these components need to be aligned and in balance. Balance refers to the alignment of the forces that create stability in our lives. This translates into the need for us to control our own personal rhythms, which leads to a healthy and successful life.

Rhythms of Habits

Human beings are creatures of habit. Habits are repetitive behaviors that fall into a rhythm or pattern. What is important about habits is that they can have positive or negative effects on the body depending on the habit. It is important to choose habits that are good for you. We develop and retain habits based on our experiences and exposure to them. They are engrained in our rhythms only if we feel that they meet our personal needs.

Take a mental trip back to your childhood years and try to identify the origins of your habits. You can also look at your personal work experiences and identify habits that have developed because of your job. You may shower in the morning or the evening or have a habit of snacking at a particular time. What about habits that you develop when you drive a particular route to work and how uncomfortable you feel if for some reason you have to take a different route. I live in Michigan, and so we live at the mercy of the orange barrels and road closures. Funny though, the roads never seem to improve despite the continued roadwork, but that has become an acceptable culture in Michigan. Once a habit has become part of your personal rhythm, it may be difficult to change or eliminate.

Some habits have a positive effect on your health, but some habits can be very dangerous to your health. For instance, smoking is a habit that is very dangerous to your health. It destroys your lungs and cardiovascular system and is responsible for cancer and pulmonary disease. Excessive alcohol ingestion and habitual overeating are also dangerous to your health. Alcohol in excess becomes a poison to the body. Overeating, another habit, can lead to obesity and the diseases.

Other habits can be good for your health, such as exercising, reading, or sleeping. These habits will make you stronger, more balanced and ultimately healthier. The first step in controlling your habits is to realize what they are and then decide if they are good for you. With this knowledge, you can begin to modify your behavioral rhythms. In cases of addictions, professional help may be needed so I encourage you to seek the help of a professional if there is something you cannot change on your own. In most cases, over time, you can make small adjustments to your personal rhythms that can change your habits and lead to a healthier you.

Relationship to Disease

So how does all of this relate to disease? It is critical to remember that our rhythms can affect our health and actually cause disease. It is important, if you want to be healthy and successful, to start focusing on including healthy lifestyle rhythms to make positive changes in your life. These rhythms include things like, stopping smoking, beginning an exercise program, reducing stress, getting enough rest, eating healthy, taking time for yourself, limiting alcohol intake, eliminating recreational drug use and beginning to care for yourself. I will show you how to do all of these later in the book but first we need to evaluate your health.

Health Risk Appraisals

One excellent tool to help you comprehensively evaluate your health is to do a health risk appraisal. A health risk appraisal will evaluate your current health status and make you aware of your risk factors for disease. This knowledge will give you some direction into what you need to change to improve your health.

Health risk appraisals may be available from the human resource department where you work. Most organizations now provide these kinds of services to employees. The Internet also has several different health risk appraisals that you can download and complete. Many of them will even provide you an evaluation. Your physician will also be a good source for the identification of a good health risk appraisal or may be able to direct you to one that is reputable.

Directions Health Evaluation Exercise

This next exercise is not a comprehensive health-risk appraisal, but it will give you some insight into your current health status. Simply answer the twenty-six questions by placing a check in either the Yes or No column. When you are finished review your results. If you have answered No to any of the questions, it may benefit you to make an appointment to see your physician or to complete a comprehensive health risk appraisal. You probably need to make some changes in your life rhythms.

CHAPTER 2 EXERCISE: HEALTH EVALUATION

Health Habits		Yes	No
1	Do you get enough sleep?		
2	Do you exercise regularly?		
3	Do you eat healthy?		
4	Do you limit your alcohol intake?		
5	Do you abstain from recreational drugs?		
6	Do you abstain from smoking?		
7	Do you control your stress?		
8	Are your family members free of disease?		
9	Do you visit your doctor regularly?		
10	Do you control your weight effectively?		
11	Do you have a normal blood pressure?		
12	Do you have normal cholesterol levels?		
13	Do you use your seatbelts?		
14	Do you drive safely?		
15	Do you practice safe sex?		
16	Do you perform self exams (i.e. Breast, Testicular)?		
17	Do you take time for any renewal activities?		
18	Do you vacation regularly?		
19	Do you have regular Pap tests? (Males leave blank)		
20	Do you have regular Prostate exams? (Females leave blank)		
21	Do you visit the dentist regularly?		
22	Do you drink enough water?		
23	Do you have smoke detectors in your home?		
24	Do you have CO_2 detectors in your home?		
25	Have you tested your home for Radon?		
26	Do you have emergency plans for your home and family?		

If you have answered No to any of these questions you may want to consider a health risk appraisal or see your physician.

Next Steps

Now that you know your personal rhythms and have an understanding of the status of your health, the next step is to look at your personal values to help you understand who you are and why you behave and think the way you do. That is the focus of our next chapter.

TAP DANCE INSTRUCTION: TAP-TAP

Here is your second step. Stand on one foot and extend the other foot. Tap the toe of the extended foot on the floor in a rhythm that accents the second tap louder than the first. It should sound like 'tap-tap'. Now, think about that rhythm. It sounds like your heartbeat, doesn't it? You can perform this as fast or as slow as you like. So, find the personal rhythm that feels good to you.

CHAPTER 3:
WHERE DO OUR RHYTHMS COME FROM?

OBJECTIVES: CHAPTER 3

1. Learn how you became you

2. Learn the meaning and power of values in your life

3. Learn how values affect your personal rhythms

4. Identify your personal values

We are now going to move in a completely different direction in regards to the study of rhythms. In the first two chapters, we learned about what rhythms are, where they are found, how they work in the universe and how they can affect our lives. We also learned that rhythms could be healthy or unhealthy and contribute to the development of disease.

This next chapter is focused on you and where your personal rhythms came from. We will learn what makes us who we are, how we establish a value system, and what does that do to the creation of our future and our personal rhythms.

What are Values?

Values are derived from our belief systems that shape our desires, behaviors, and aspirations for what we want to do with our lives. Values are not right or wrong they are simply a part of who we are. All of us possess particular value systems that are uniquely different from each other and those values can change over time. The changes are a result of exposure to circumstances or experiences throughout our lives.

The difference in values can account for the synergy as well as tension that we find in our lives and more globally in our society. Can you imagine what it would be like if we all had the same set values or if we all had the same belief system? It would be incredibly boring. We would have no excitement or diversity in our lives. We would all think alike, desire the same things, and function the same way, somewhat like a Stepford Wife approach to life.

As a society, we share many common values and beliefs. Freedom is a common value that we share in our country, but the intensity of our values and behaviors may vary greatly between individuals. For instance, let's look at the value of achievement. Some people are high achievers whereby others may not share the same level of drive. Collaboration is another common value that is shared with great variability. Some people like to work with others, and some people like to work alone. You probably can identify people like this in your work setting. Most people value friendship; however there are those who claim that they don't have friends nor do they need them. What about humor? I'm sure you have worked with people or have been around people that are funny and enjoyable to be with because they incorporate humor into their lives. Integrity is another strong value that can guide behaviors. There are examples all through the media that identify individuals that lack integrity. Other values may include things like personal development, pleasure, and recognition. Religion is a very strong value system in our culture for most people as is self-respect. These values frame who you are and ultimately guide your behavior.

Where do Values Come From?

Values can arise from a variety of sources. As children, values can be established by our learning and growth process. Therefore our early values come from our childhood experiences with many of them originating from the core values of our parents. I am sure you remember all of those old sayings designed to keep you in line. Do your homework, clean your room, don't talk back, say please and thank you, say you're sorry, and don't hit your little brother are all expressions driven by a set of core values that your parents subscribed to. They were instilling values to drive your behavior throughout life.

Both of my parents were schoolteachers. The fact that they believed in the value of education led to this strong value in my siblings and me. Perhaps that is why I continued pursuing advanced degrees and have committed myself to a journey of lifelong learning. In other words, my parents' value of education molded my behavior and probably much of my success. They were also very religious so faith and religion became core values during those early years that have remained with me into adulthood.

Values also come from our personal experiences. If you have had a brush with death or are facing the challenges of a serious disease, you may have a little bit different appreciation for life, or a little more respect for your health than someone who has not had that experience.

I have been a director of critical care and emergency services for many years. I could always identify values in a nurse by observing them caring for patients. They seem to have a deeper sense of empathy and compassion in dealing with death and dying if they have had a personal experience with death or loss in their own families. They could put themselves in the shoes of the people that were experiencing a personal tragedy. I also observed that nurses who were parents related more intimately with the parents of children that had died or were seriously ill. That is not to say that all of our nurses were not effective in their communication with patients, all of them do a wonderful job. In my experience, there seems to be a deeper understanding of pain and sorrow, which translates to the communication patterns with the patients and families.

Alignment of values with behaviors

Now that you know about values, it is important to realize that values need to be aligned with our behaviors and personal rhythms in order for us to feel good about ourselves and be successful. There are several leadership publications that address the concept of alignment as a critical success factor in all we do in our jobs, careers, and personal goals.

Here is another example to ponder. I am taking you back to hospital examples because that happens to be my past, but you can translate any of these examples and place them in the context of your work or personal experiences.

Earlier in my nursing administration experience, I was responsible for merging two hospitals into one "hopefully" big happy family. Those of you, whether you are in a hospital system or not, know that mergers and acquisitions are always very stressful for the staff affected and never are a welcomed experience. Even healthy mergers that eventually lead to strong organizations begin with fear and turmoil. Cultural issues and a lack of quality leadership may lead some of these organizations to fail.

In my personal experience, in relation to our discussion of values, one of these hospitals was Catholic and the other was not. As we mentioned before, the value of religion is one of the strongest and most endearing. The hospital that I worked in was the non-Catholic hospital and also the purchasing organization. Although we had many examples of culture clashes throughout the organization, there was one very profound misalignment of values that was difficult to overcome in the context of this merger resulting in the loss of nursing staff. My organization performed abortions in the obstetrical department, which were prohibited by the faith-based organization. This created incredible conflict with many of the nurses in the faith based organization since they were now expected to practice outside their belief system. Although we did not expect them to alter their values and perform the abortions, many of them could not accept the fact that the hospital was going to continue to perform them. This resulted in many nurses struggling with a choice that did not feel good to them causing a percentage of them to seek employment elsewhere.

Regardless of the circumstance, it is vital that you remain true to your values and that those values are aligned with behaviors and choices in your life whether that be in your job, family, or personal situations. This also demonstrates the strength of commitment to your personal values. At times, we find ourselves in situations that create conflict and cause us to struggle with personal dilemmas. Perhaps you work with a boss that you don't agree with in regards to work ethic or practice. Maybe you have a friend that's trying to lead you down the wrong path or a friend that engages in behaviors that you don't agree with. All of these situations can cause conflict in your life since they are not aligned with your personal values.

Directions Values Analysis Exercise

We are now going to do an exercise to help you identify your personal values. Listed in alphabetical order is a list of common values. You will need to make some tough decisions here since you will find that you probably subscribe to many of these values although in varying degrees. We are going to force rank these so that you choose the values you feel most represent you.

First of all, read through the list. Select six that you feel most represent you. Review them again and rank them from number one, being your strongest, to number six, being your weakest. It may also be insightful to you to have someone else do this analysis for you such as a spouse or significant other to see how he or she perceives you. Oftentimes, we have perceptions about ourselves that may be different than the perceptions of others. If you are true to your values, what you should find is that everyone else who does this exercise for you will select the same values or those that are close to the choices you have made. If there is misalignment, you may need to change your situations that lead to personal conflict and misalignment.

Once you know what your values are, you can begin to analyze and craft behaviors that fit your values. Your values can then provide you a roadmap to create your personal mission statement to guide you through life.

For the next part of this exercise, after you have chosen your six values in order from one to six, next to the value identify behaviors or activities that you think will help you remain consistent with that value.

For instance, if you've chosen education (going back to my life), some behaviors that you could exhibit that would help you achieve this goal are things like going back to school. Maybe you want to finish a degree. Maybe you want to take the time to read more or maybe you want to take a class in an area of interest for you. Maybe you have knowledge to share with others, so you may want to teach a class. Regardless of your choice of activity, as long as you are teaching or learning, you are aligned with your value of education.

I recently did this with a group of employees to identify the team's core values. This exercise can be very effective with teams that you work with in that it can align thinking and find common ground needed for accomplishing goals. One value that this particular team chose was integrity. Some of the supporting behaviors that they identified to support this value in their work environment were things like curtailing gossip, always being honest with each other, and providing support when necessary. They also pledged to not speak negatively about each other and to be open with their feelings. The outcome following this exercise was a team that was committed to the goal but more importantly, committed to each other.

Once you complete this exercise, contemplate the information and identify how you may apply it. The next step is to write a personal mission statement for you. In the next chapter we will begin to work on goals and objectives to fulfill your values and help you align your life and rhythms.

CHAPTER 3 EXERCISE: VALUES ANALYSIS

Values Analysis: Check

Achievement (attaining goals, feeling of accomplishment) _____

Advancement (growth of department and each other) _____

Adventure (willing to take risks, try new processes) _____

Competition (strive to be the best) _____

Collaboration (work well with others) _____

Economic Stability (balance budget, cost conscious) _____

Education (school, learning) _____

Empowerment (able to contribute and make relevant decisions) _____

Fairness (treat everyone the same, review all situations) _____

Family (focus on any family members) _____

Friendship (close relationship with each other) _____

Health (self care, health habits, exercise, nutrition) _____

Helpfulness (willing to assist each other) _____

Humor (believe in the power of laughter) _____

Inclusion (desires to be included with others) _____

Integrity (high level of honesty, true to beliefs) _____

Involvement (active participation with others) _____

Loyalty (committed to department and role) _____

Order (believe in the need for organization and structure) _____

Perseverance (strength despite challenges) _____

Personal Development (help each other to improve and grow) _____

Pleasure (strive to make the job fun) _____

Power (influence, importance, authority) _____

Recognition (receive and give acknowledgement) _____

Religion (strong belief in faith) _____

Relationships (belief in the need for relationships) _____

Responsibility (accountable, reliable) _____

Self-Respect (self-esteem, believe in the team) _____

Spirituality (possess a belief in faith) _____

Teamwork (work together, support all team members) _____

Wealth (desire more resources) _____

Wisdom (support knowledge and education) _____

Values and Personal Mission

To help illustrate how our values will fold into the direction of our lives, I will share with you my values and mission. What was interesting to me was the fact that three basic values have not changed throughout my life. The priorities and focus, however, have changed based on various situations and stages in my life.

Health happens to be my first and most important core value. It is my belief that without good health, I will not be able to fulfill my life's mission. This value has probably guided my choices to pursue a degree in nursing and also to write this book. The behaviors that I have identified and practiced to help me achieve my goal to stay healthy are exercising daily, maintaining a steady weight, and regularly taking part in renewal activities.

My second core value is family. I have a very strong belief that family is very important to a happy life. The behaviors that support this value are expressing love and support for my family and putting them first. I also feel that it is valuable to coach and support my kids to help them reach their personal goals.

The third value is that of education. In fulfillment of this value I have completed my doctoral degree, wrote this book, taught many courses and classes, and provide mentorship to the staff in my work setting. I also love to speak publicly and continue to teach dance and exercise classes, which are also expressions of my value for education. As long as I am engaged in an activity that promotes learning, I am aligned with my personal value of education.

Personal Mission Statement

Evaluation of your values in the context of your life will help you to identify your personal mission statement. Experts say that a mission statement should be short and concise. It should be short enough to fit on a t-shirt and concise enough for you to easily remember. My personal mission statement is simply, "To help others be the best that they can be."

Mission Statement Applications

Now, a simple mission statement is easy to incorporate into your life. For instance, I can apply my mission statement to helping my kids or my whole family and friends. I can also use it to help drive my behaviors in my work environment and in my writing and teaching. The last portion of the exercise is to finish writing your personal mission statement.

Next Steps

Now that you understand your personal values and have identified your personal mission statement, the next step will be to identify goals to help you fulfill your mission on earth. That is the focus of our next chapter.

TAP DANCE INSTRUCTION: BRUSH BACK AND FORTH

Here is your third tap step. We spoke of how values provide the background for your life so our tap step will do the same. Standing on one leg, slide your toe back and forth creating a dragging brushing sound that represents the background noise of values in your life.

CHAPTER 4:
ALL ABOUT GOALS

OBJECTIVES: CHAPTER 4

1. Learn about goal setting

2. Learn why goals are necessary in our lives

3. Learn how to identify goals and align them with your values

4. Develop your life goal statements

What are Goals?

George Zalucki said *that the mind needs what he calls specific intent (which is a goal), in order to function as an optimum achievement mechanism.* In other words, we need goals in our lives to provide structure and direction. These goals help contribute to our personal growth, achievement and ultimately become key drivers of our unique personal rhythms and behaviors.

Alfred Adler believed that the creative power of life is expressed through the process of identifying, developing, working toward and achieving goals. We all need goals. If we have no goals, we lose our focus, we feel lost, we have no direction, and this will lead to frustration and make it difficult for us to achieve our desired success.

I had the opportunity to read an incredibly compelling book when I was in my doctoral program, called *Man's Search of Meaning* by Viktor Frankl. Dr. Frankl was a psychiatrist who believed that without goals men would give up hope and die. He based his theories on his own personal experience as a prisoner of war in several concentration camps during World War II. He described how he watched people die in the camps when they lost their hope and meaning in their life. He found that this loss of hope seemed to be most devastating when the prisoners had to face the reality that their families were gone because of the atrocities of this time. He described how he kept himself alive by establishing goals and looking for meaning, which drove the behaviors, which were necessary for him to survive. One of his goals was to share what he learned about goals and human behavior by writing a book after his release. He wanted to help others through his observations and writings. The book described how he focused on the end product and began writing notes while he was imprisoned on anything that he could scratch words on. This focus gave him an opportunity to channel his mental thought processes to something positive amidst an environment of living hell.

The focus of this chapter is to help you identify your goals to provide a roadmap for your success. Developing your goals will help you organize your experiences and direct your action toward your desired outcomes. When you drive a car, you need to know your destination and then how to get there. You would not think of traveling by car without a map or way to navigate new roads. Many people, however, manage through life without direction. Your goals provide you a road map to achievement. This road map will then help you to begin to align your actions in the direction of your goals.

Strategies for Goal Success

There are several proven strategies to improve the quality of goal setting and the resulting success of reaching those goals. It is important to remember to...

1. Align your goals with your personal values (we did this in chapter three).

2. Write your goals down, this makes a visible contract with yourself.

3. Set reasonable deadlines that you think you can accomplish.

4. Make sure that your goals are measurable so you can chart your progress.

5. Celebrate your accomplishments. Be proud of your successes!

Aligning Goals With Values

The first step for developing your goals is to align those goals with your personal values. If your goals do not align with your values, as we mentioned before, you will have continued conflict in your life and difficulty achieving the goal.

A dear friend of mine went to medical school to be a physician only because his father pressured him to follow in his footsteps. His father kept telling him that it would be an insult to him if he didn't become a doctor as he had. Under this tremendous pressure, he went through the motions. He went to medical school, did his residency, and did very well throughout the program. He was at the top of his class and could have had any position he wanted upon completion. The big problem for him was that medicine was not his passion. It did not align with his value system and what he wanted to do with his life. After a great deal of soul searching, he decided that he could no longer live with this internal conflict. He realized that he was living out his father's dream and not his. He decided to leave the medical profession and pursue a different degree. He ended up studying law and now focuses on malpractice law. For him, this was a way to use his medical degree yet pursue a career of interest. His father has yet to forgive him but he feels that it was far more important to be true to his values. He now feels that in his current role he is helping people by being their voice of advocacy.

This is a great example of the importance of proper goal alignment. We oftentimes try to inflict our personal goals and aspirations on others so that we can feel vicariously successful. In my experience as a dance instructor, I have observed the typical "stage mom" who continually pushes their child to do better because of the perception that the daughter's performance is a direct reflection on themselves. I have had mothers become very upset if their daughter was not in the front line, if they didn't have a solo or if they didn't look good in the costume I had chosen. At times, this behavior can become oppressive and destructive for the child. I have always been careful not to put this type of pressure on my kids but to allow them to experience different opportunities to be able to select what is good for them. (Of course, you know kids, they will probably believe something different.)

Writing Goals Down

Writing down your goals transforms them from a mere thought to tangible evidence, which ultimately makes them real to you. This then becomes your target to direct your behaviors. The written document also gives you the opportunity to review them and measure your progress. Write your goals down and review them frequently. Write down both your short and long term goals. Short-term goals are things that can be achieved very quickly. For example, I find that I am much more effective when I get up in the morning and write down all that I want to accomplish for the day on a list. These are all short-term goals. Throughout the day I periodically go back to the list and cross off what I have accomplished and look at what still needs to be completed. At the end of the day, I can actually see all that I have achieved. I find that this type of organization through the use of short-term goals actually provides me more free time because I find that I am more efficient and driven. I channel my behaviors toward the completion of the daily goals that I have identified. This also helps me feel that I am in control of my time.

Long-term goals are a little different from short-term goals in that they will take longer to complete, sometimes years. They might include things like achieving your dream career, completing an academic degree, buying a house or car, or losing weight. What about self-improvement or developing relationships? Whatever your goals are put them in writing and look at them regularly. Reviewing them will help you develop strategies and change course to keep you on track. In the next couple chapters, we will be developing your goals and creating a plan that becomes a living document that will guide you in your journey toward great outcomes.

Reasonable Deadlines

You have to be reasonable with your timelines for goal achievement, so you need to set reasonable deadlines. Setting a deadline is like signing a contract. You have now made a commitment through a timeline for completion. If your goal is to lose weight, you want to set a reasonable deadline based on how much you want to lose and how much time you can dedicate to your goal. It is reasonable and healthy to expect to lose one to two pounds per week. If your goal is to lose twenty pounds, you could safely achieve that in eight weeks. If you set an unrealistic goal to lose twenty pounds in two weeks, you have already set yourself up for failure. First of all, it is not healthy to attempt that degree of weight loss, but most importantly, it is something that cannot be accomplished.

As a personal trainer, I would receive calls from people who wanted to lose weight in time for an event that was only a couple of weeks away. I actually received a call from a wife of a well-known sports star to lose an unrealistic amount of weight for cosmetic reasons prior to a very important party. She was willing to pay me a great deal of money if I would be able to help her. I declined the offer knowing that this goal was not reasonable, and neither she nor I would be successful. She did find someone to work with her and she did not lose the weight. The moral of the story is that with goal setting it is critically important for you to have the chance to be successful and feel good about your accomplishments. If not, you may feel demoralized which may lead to your reluctance to take risks and attempt other goals.

Goals Should be Measurable

One way to help you continually monitor your success is to make goals measurable. How will you know that you've achieved your goal if you can't measure it? Nebulous goals are out there like clouds in the sky; they are fluffy without structure. You can't grab clouds, you can't hold them, and you will never be able to identify a strategy to move toward them. Goals such as "I want a happy life," are nebulous and moving targets since the definition of happiness, to many people, changes over time. The reality is that achieving your goals and aligning your personal values and rhythms will ultimately make you happy, but setting a goal such as this will not provide you any direction. You will need to identify individual goals that upon accomplishment will make you happy.

If you have set a goal, for instance, of achieving wealth, you need to identify what wealth means to you and how much money you would like to make. You can then channel your behaviors in the appropriate direction. For instance, you may want to find a job that pays more within the next two years. Now your goal is measurable. Within two years, it is possible to achieve a promotion or find a better job. Completing my doctoral degree by age 50 was measurable. Finishing the laundry on Saturday is measurable. Taking a class in September is measurable.

Another advantage to having specific measurable guidelines is that if you are not achieving your goal as quickly as you would like, you can change your strategy.

Celebrate Your Success

Celebration is a formal way to recognize accomplishments and a ritual that validates your success. It is a very important step in affirmation of achieving your goals. How good did you feel when you graduated and walked to receive your diploma? How good did you feel when you celebrated at your wedding, or how important is the recognition of a birthday? These are all examples of celebrations that validate success. It is important to take time to enjoy the moment through celebration.

Here is a great example of the importance of celebration. For many years, I was a personal trainer in my spare time. I had a client who was a delightful lady that wanted to lose fifty pounds. She set her goal and was determined to make this important change in her life. She developed her timeline and planned to measure her progress through weight loss and clothing size. To help her with this commitment, she wrote everything down. Within six months, she lost the weight, looked fabulous and felt wonderfully in control of her life. She decided that in order to celebrate she would buy herself a gold belly-chain to wear underneath her clothes everyday as a continual reminder of her new waistline. It also provided ongoing motivation to help her keep the weight off. I lost track of her several years after she achieved her goal. I met her in a grocery store five years later, and she still looked fabulous! After the hugs and small talk, she lifted her shirt up a little and showed me the belly chain that she had been wearing for five years. For her, the ability to wear the chain represented her success. It was a way to remind herself of all the commitment, hard work and her desire to keep the weight off. Even more importantly, it continually reaffirmed her perseverance and personal strength, which she believed was what prevented her from returning to old habits.

Directions: *Identify Your Goals*

Now it is time to identify the goals that align with your values. The first step is to go back to your values assessment and review your top three. Three goals are usually enough to work on so don't over subscribe by trying to work on too many at one time.

Using the tool, write down your top three values then next to them write down one major goal that meets the intent of the value. It can be anything that you want to accomplish. For instance, if one of your core values is education, your corresponding goal might be to complete a degree. Whatever the choice, write it down. If your value is health and you want to lose weight, write it down. Remember that when we identify goals they need to align with your core values.

CHAPTER 4 EXERCISE: IDENTIFYING YOUR GOALS

Core Value	Corresponding Goal	Time-line	Comments

Next Steps

Now that you know your values and have identified some major goals for your life, the next step is to begin to develop your strategy to get there. We will do this through the use of objectives, which are tasks and behaviors necessary to accomplish your goals.

TAP DANCE INSTRUCTION: RUNNING FLAPS

Here is your next step. We are now beginning to make great progress toward your goals and are running in the right direction! This next step is called running flaps. To make the sound, you stay on your toe and begin to run forward. While you do this relax your ankle and drop the toe to allow it to brush on the floor and create two sounds. It should sound like 'flap-tap, flap-tap'. Alternate from right to left.

CHAPTER 5:
ALL ABOUT OBJECTIVES

OBJECTIVES: CHAPTER 5

1. Learn about objectives

2. Learn how to write objectives that align with personal goals

3. Learn how to put objectives into action

What are Objectives?

Now that you have identified major goals that you wish to accomplish, it is time to create the roadmap to get there. Objectives are that roadmap. Think of goals as what you want to accomplish and think of objectives as how to get there. In order for objectives to be effective, they need to be very detailed and measurable, with definite outcomes and timelines. They should also be written as action items that are to be completed.

Writing Objectives

The first step in writing objectives is to review and think about your goal. Once you understand the goal and know what it is you want to accomplish, start thinking of the individual steps you need to take to get you there. Now you are ready to begin writing the steps down. For instance, if your goal is to get married six months from now, you need to plan a wedding. To begin you need to develop a list of objectives that must to be accomplished. This list of objectives would include things like: set the date, schedule the church, schedule the hall, arrange for music, select a caterer, select and order flowers, order the invitations, select the wedding party, purchase the wedding dress, order centerpieces, select dresses for the bridesmaids, photographer, rehearsal dinner, and on and on and on.

Once you have your list of objectives write them in an action statement to be acted upon. Let's look at the first objective, which is to set the date. In order to set the date you will need to perform some actions such as review the calendar for desirable dates, talk to your fiancé, perhaps talk to your family, and then finally select the date. To choose your wedding dress you may want to begin with action items such as a review of wedding magazines, a visit to local bridal shops, scheduling the fitting, etc. This practice should be repeated for all of your objectives until you complete your whole work plan. This list of objectives is now your roadmap to help you achieve your goal of planning your wedding.

Another important step is to assign target dates by which you need to complete the tasks. For instance, in our wedding planning example, many of the objectives have longer lead times such as scheduling the hall or ordering the dress and invitations. Target dates will help you complete the tasks in the appropriate timeframe to meet your deadlines. This will help you especially if you tend to procrastinate. People who procrastinate oftentimes live in a world of chaos with deadlines closing in on them.

Once you write all of the information in your document, review it often to see where you are in the process, what progress you have made toward your goal, and how far you still need to go. Life happens so there will be times you need to change course, slow down, or speed up the activity. You need to be flexible and respond to the need to change course when necessary. This is also another reason to frequently review your document.

Other Applications for Goals and Objectives

Setting goals and objectives are beneficial in other settings as well. You can use this approach whenever there is a need for strategic planning. If you are the leader of an organization or a leader of a team, you can apply this practice of goal setting to achieve success of an organization or team. Maybe you lead your child's basketball team or a community organization. You can formally set goals to achieve a winning team or projects for your group. This process is applicable for any setting where outcomes can be improved by planning and organization.

There are several success factors to help you with writing effective objectives. These include the importance of relating your objectives to your goals, keeping your objectives achievable, making your goals and objectives a living document, and sharing your desires with others. Let's discuss all of these.

Relate Objectives to Your Goal

First of all, you must relate the objectives to the goal. Just as it is important to align your goals to your personal values, it is just as important to make sure that your objectives align with your goal. Be very concise and choose only the objectives that you think will move you toward your goal. You need to focus your energies in the right direction.

Keep Your Objectives Achievable

The second success factor is to select objectives that are achievable. For instance, if you want to lose weight and begin an exercise program, you might choose a gym membership as an objective. You may then decide to go to the gym seven days a week for three hours. Well, you will probably do that for the first two days. This aggressive goal would be impossible for almost everyone so, by choosing this schedule, you have set yourself up for certain failure. In this case, you may want to begin by saying that you will go to the gym three times a week for an hour. Now, this objective becomes more achievable instead of a very lofty stretch goal. You have turned it into something very manageable for yourself. Once you begin your program, you can adjust you schedule to visit the gym more frequently if you can fit that in your schedule.

Make Your Goals and Objectives a Living Document

You want to make this a living document, one that you review on a regular basis. When you are finished identifying your values, goals, objectives, and tasks, you'll have a comprehensive roadmap for your success. The reality, however, is that people and circumstances change and for whatever reason, our goals may change. You should plan on reviewing and updating your plan frequently, at least monthly. If things change in your life, simply revise your plan. Use the comment section to keep important notes and to document when the task is completed. This is a great way to realize all the things that you have accomplished as well as continue to move forward.

Share Your Plan with Others

It is beneficial to share your goals and objectives with others. It may be your spouse, significant other, a close friend or family member. Those who care about you may be able to provide you the valuable support you need to keep going. I reflect back to the tough decision to put my life on hold to finish my last degree. I discussed this first with my husband since I knew that he and the family would have to make some significant sacrifices for me to realize my goal. He was very willing to help me (as always) and was there to pick up the slack at home when I was buried with assignments. We as a family just did what we all needed to do for me to finish my program. To this day, I look back at that time and wonder how I managed to do that. The answer is with the help of my family. Solicit the help of others. We are all here to help each other get through life but unless we ask the questions, others may never know what we are thinking or what we secretly desire.

Sharing your plan with others will also help improve your accountability to your commitment. There are more than just your eyes on the target and more people watching your progress. You also won't want to let your family or friends down since you will know that they want you to succeed.

If you have some professional goals that relate to your work, you may want to share them with your boss or a mentor at work. I always enjoy when one of my staff members comes to me to share their professional goals. I feel that this demonstrates an individual who has a grasp of what they want to achieve, and I always make it a point to help them in any way I can. I also feel privileged that they have shared their thoughts with me because I perceive that they respect my opinion. So don't be afraid to ask for help. You will be surprised how often you will receive it.

Directions: Writing Your Objectives

Your activity for this chapter is going to be to build your comprehensive personal strategic plan. The template is self-explanatory. Across the top, you have objectives, initiatives, target date and comments. At the top is room for you to include your goal. Go back to your original goal and write in Goal 1. In the first column, write your 'objective one,' 'objective two,' and 'objective three.' Fill in the initiatives that you feel you need to accomplish the objectives. Fill in the target date and any comments that you feel are important to record.

If you chose to do more than one goal, repeat the entire exercise with another template. Now it's time to start filling in your plan and building a roadmap to future success.

CHAPTER 5 EXERCISE:
WRITING YOUR OBJECTIVES

Goal #1:

Objective	Initiative	Target Date	Comments

Goal #2:

Objective	Initiative	Target Date	Comments

Goal #3:			
Objective	**Initiative**	**Target Date**	**Comments**

Next Steps

Congratulations! You know who you are, why you are the way you are, and now have a great idea of what you want out of life through these past exercises. You also have developed a strategic set of goals and objectives to move you toward your success. The next chapter will focus on our minds and our mental rhythms and begin to give you the fundamentals of harnessing the mind and body to be the best we can be.

TAP DANCE INSTRUCTION: FLAP TOE HEEL

The tap step for this chapter is called the Alternating Flap Toe Heel. We are becoming a bit more intricate. Lightly brush the toe forward on the floor (flap) place the toe on the ground (toe) and then drop the heel (heel drop). Repeat this in an alternating fashion from right to left. Practice speeding this up and slowing it down as well as changing the rhythms.

CHAPTER 6:
THE POWER & RHYTHM OF POSITIVE THINKING

OBJECTIVES: CHAPTER 6

1. Learn the power of positive thinking

2. Learn the importance of positive mental processing

3. Learn how the mind can affect the body

4. Learn how to transfer thoughts into actions

5. Learn the difference between the conscious and subconscious mind

6. Become aware of your personal thought rhythms and how you can change them to your advantage.

Importance of Positive Thinking

It has been said that what calls us to action in our lives is desire, but what helps us achieve our goals is the belief in ourselves that we can accomplish the goal. This belief in ourselves is called self-efficacy. If we believe we can achieve it, then we are always right. If we believe we cannot achieve it, we are also always right. So, the choice becomes yours.

This chapter is all about concepts and tools to achieve your goals and to fulfill your deepest desires. The greatest tool you have is the power of positive thinking. What sounds so simple is really very difficult for many people. By learning your thought rhythms, however, you can change them to create the attitude you need to help you believe in yourself and be a success.

Research has now shown a very strong correlation between positive thinking practices and successful personal outcomes. Studies of people one hundred years old and older reveal that those who are happy and perceive themselves successful have one thing in common; they are positive about their future no matter how old they are.

Similar studies on individuals with disease suggest that stress and negative thought processes are habitual patterns for them. You may know people like this. Have you ever had a friend that is always complaining? Nothing is ever right. Their cup is always half empty. Everything is a big problem to them. It may also be your experience that these people are not fun to be around and actually bring you down to their level of misery when they are with you. You don't need to choose these types of friends nor should you subject yourself to negative energy.

In my experience over the years in several leadership positions, I have found that many times, negative people are impossible to influence. I like to use the saying that if I gave these individuals a million dollars, they would complain it is not in twenty-dollar bills. I realize that I am describing the extreme, but if we look into our own behaviors we may have some of these negative thought tendencies holding us back. Understanding our mental thought patterns can help us make a change. As we have discussed before, awareness is always the first step to personal change.

Thought Rhythms

Thought rhythms are habitual ways of thinking that affect all we do in our lives. They tie into our value and belief systems and actually direct our behaviors. To understand this phenomenon, we need to understand four different concepts, the conscious mind, the subconscious mind, energy theories, and thoughts as realities.

The Conscious Mind

The conscious mind is linked to our sympathetic nervous system and is the thought rhythm that we are the most familiar with. This is the part of the mind that results in the chatter that you constantly hear in your head. A good friend of mind who is an integrative medicine specialist refers to this as your monkey mind that constantly chatters and talks to you. Ever had one of those nights where you couldn't fall asleep? The mind races and talks and talks and talks. This is your chattering monkey mind. It is often referred to as the back of your mind, you are always consciously thinking while in an awakened state.

Take a few minutes at this time to sit quietly and attempt to remove all thoughts from your mind. Can you make your mind a total blank? Not for long—the chatter kicks in and you begin to think and talk to yourself. You may be thinking, 'wow, this is interesting,' or 'I didn't know that.' You may be thinking about how am I going to accomplish a task, or what am I going to do tomorrow? The conscious mind therefore is the most dominant, but unfortunately is also the mind that is full of self-doubt. These are the questions you continually ask yourself: Can I do it? Will I be successful? Am I good enough? These negative thoughts have several origins that begin to create thought patterns. The conscious mind creates negative thoughts based on our fears and past experiences. Most of the time, these feelings and beliefs are very hard to overcome however, *they can be!*

How many times have you forgotten something or have done something wrong that resulted in a self-talk phrases such as, 'I'm so stupid.' Have you ever looked in the mirror and thought that you were fat? What about the all-time favorite, 'I could never do that'? Some of these phrases may be familiar to you. You probably have an expanded collection of your own thoughts that you repeatedly use as personal assaults on yourself. Would you ever say something like that to your husband or wife or someone you really cared for? How about, "Honey, you are so fat"? Well, not if you want to stay married, but you wouldn't say those things to people you care about. What is amazing is that we never think twice about using these verbal assaults on ourselves.

We also may pick up negative thoughts along the way from others in our lives. Perhaps your parents called you stupid or placed demands on you that you thought were impossible. Maybe your siblings contributed to some of your negative beliefs. What about your friends or experiences in school? The incidence of teen suicide continues to escalate with the type of pressures that students are facing from their relationships and the treatment they receive from others.

The Unconscious Mind

Our subconscious or unconscious mind is linked to what we call the parasympathetic nervous system. It works behind the scenes to take what we believe and learn through the course of our lives and turn it into our personal reality. This is the part of the mind that does not talk back to you and has no judgment capability. Some people call this intuition or the sixth sense. The knowledge is there in the background, but it may not be apparent to you.

Remember that our conscious mind is always processing thoughts and evaluating truth and what is real to us. The subconscious mind, on the other hand, does not have any judgment capability, but rather acts like a supercomputer that is programmed by your conscious mind. Think about this for a moment. In other words, our conscious mind continuously sends messages to our subconscious mind, which then programs our behaviors to fulfill those beliefs. The unconscious mind cannot challenge the beliefs but rather simply sets the behaviors into actions. Your subconscious mind does not have the ability to say, "That's not true!" Here is an example.

Obesity is a problem for many people in our country and continues to be one of the major causes of disease. Let's say that you may have some concern about your weight. You are unhappy with the way you look or feel, so whenever you look in the mirror you repeat statements like, "I'm so fat. I will never lose this weight." Or, "I have no will power." These

CHAPTER SIX - THE POWER & RHYTHM OF POSITIVE THINKING

are all negative verbal assaults on you. Consciously, you tell yourself this until you program this in your subconscious, and then it becomes one of your subconscious core beliefs. What is happening behind the scene is that your subconscious mind, which has no judgment capabilities, says, "Okay, I'm fat." Now the body is programmed to achieve the core belief it's fat. Whether that is through overeating or not exercising the body will respond to the program in the subconscious mind.

Now, if the reverse is true and you start to tell yourself that you are in control of your life or you are at your ideal weight, you will reprogram your subconscious mind to maintain that desired condition. The body will do whatever you program it to do. Your thoughts become reality that shapes your behaviors and attitudes.

As I was beginning to climb the corporate ladder in various leadership positions, one of my great mentors told me that I should never dress for the position I have but rather dress for the position I wish to have. My mentor believed that dressing for success helps to program the mind and create a state of readiness to perform the behaviors consistent with the next level position. She also said that your appearance affects those around you, especially those who have the power to promote you. I adopted that practice, began wearing business suits, and always dressed for a position above the position I was in. I am not suggesting that this practice was the only reason for my promotions over the years, but it helped me to program my thought processes toward behaviors consistent with advanced positions and probably had some influence on those who had promoted me. In my experience with hiring and promoting individuals over a thirty-five year career, someone who attends an interview in a business suit, regardless of the level of job, sends a strong message that they are serious about the job and are respectful of my authority. Show up in jeans and a T-shirt with flip-flops and you have sent the complete opposite message.

Why Thoughts Are So Powerful

As scientists become more fascinated and interested in the power of the human mind, research is beginning to produce some interesting evidence.

The notion of the process of thought is more tangible than what we have believed in the past. There are theories and evidence to suggest that memories are actually stored in the cells and passed on genetically, sometimes over centuries of time.

For instance, how does a body heal an injury? If you have a cut on your hand you don't need to tell your body to heal the injury. The cells do it all by themselves because they are programmed and have the memory to do that. Are the cells actually thinking? As I mentioned before, several years ago, I was a victim of a mountain bike accident that resulted in the crushing injuries of my left arm and wrist. I had four pins, an external fixator, two surgeries and about a year of physical therapy. My arm and wrist x-rays today are almost identical to my x-rays prior to the injury. The x-ray immediately following the injury showed the bones crushed to bits with an arm significantly shorter than the unaffected arm. How did my body heal so amazingly? And how did the pieces come back together in such a perfect way? Could it be the notion of cellular intelligence that cells really can think and act independent of the conscious mind? That is the focus of some startling research. One theory is that memories are stored in the cell, in the form of what we call a thought, or now know as a thought form. This can be transferred genetically, but it is also believed that our thought forms may be a result of past experiences, our values (as we've talked about before), and our learned behaviors all of which guide our personal rhythms.

Think of your favorite place in the world to be. Close your eyes and visualize the setting. It is amazing how clearly you can see the mental picture. If you concentrate on this picture enough, you may also be able to sense smells and sounds associated with the setting along with experienced feelings. These are all a result of thought forms that reconstruct the pictures for your review whenever you want. Perhaps you see a lost love from the past or a pet that has died. You remember what your children were like when they were young. These are complements of the thought forms in your mind.

These memories also convey messages to your body based on the emotions and fears that are associated with the memories themselves.

These physical reactions can have a positive or negative effect on the body. We will spend some time on these in the next chapter. So, tuck this idea away for now.

Energy Theories

Thought forms are energy, in fact, we are nothing but energy. All of our molecules are held together by energy within our own energy fields, which resides in the larger energy field of the universe. If you would look at your hand under an electron microscope, you would not recognize your hand, but rather a collection of molecules, and smaller yet, atoms held together by energy. This concept is very well studied and understood within the science of quantum physics. There is a good deal of press surrounding the concept of the law of attraction. This law suggests that your thoughts, which are energy, send messages as energy to the universe attracting and creating the results of the thought energies. In other words, you receive from the universe what you think. Whether these results are perceived positively or negatively depend on the receiver. This further supports the idea that you are what you think. Proponents of this law suggest that if you focus on the negative, you receive negative while focusing on the positive brings you more positive.

How to Keep Your Thoughts Positive

Staying positive at times seems impossible; however, there are some strategies to help you take those negative thoughts and turn them into positives. These include lowering your expectations, not giving into negative thoughts, being grateful, refraining from comparing yourself to others, and surrounding yourself with positive people.

Keep Your Expectations Reasonable

The first success factor is to keep your expectations reasonable. One practice that ensures failure is setting very high expectations that may be difficult or impossible to achieve. It is far better to set reasonable expectations that can become more challenging over time while following smaller successes. I have an example of a friend who is always happy regardless of the circumstances. When asked how she can be happy all the time the response is that she sets her expectations at a very basic level. She views waking up every morning as a gift of an opportunity to live another day. This frames the day, early in the morning, by creating a positive perspective. Think about your expectations and see if you may be falling into the trap of unrealistic expectations that could be creating frustration in your life.

Look at Every Experience as Positive

Every experience in the end is a good experience. It may not feel that way when we are experiencing pain, but we learn from each experience and oftentimes the learning is more profound with negative experiences. When you experience a painful situation, instead of reacting negatively or engaging in negative self-talk, ask yourself the question, "What am I supposed to learn from this?" In the long run, you will find a way to appreciate the good in every single learning experience even though it may take time for you to realize the benefits.

Even in cases of personal loss, we can take the experience and ultimately create a positive outcome by our actions such as helping others. There are several examples of people that have taken terrible experiences and turned them into positive ways to help others. The Amber Alert, Mothers Against Drunk Driving, and S.A.D.D. (Students Against Disastrous Decisions) are examples of tragedy whereby the negative energy was channeled to do good for others. In my current organization, we have suicide support groups for parents who have lost children taught by parents who have experienced this tragedy. It is a way for them to help others cope through these tough times and eventually return to some degree of comfort and normalcy in their lives.

Many key phrases that I have used to help me persevere through tough times have come from my mother. She always told me that, "This too shall pass," and "time heals all." I have found that this is true in all of my past experiences.

Change Negative Thoughts to Positive Affirmations

It is easy to fall into the trap of habitual negative thinking. The first step to changing this practice is to be aware of what we are saying to ourselves. These negative thoughts affect our lives and tear away our self-confidence and reap havoc with our personal belief system. Once we know our negative thought rhythms, we can learn to spin them into positive affirmations.

For instance, are you not doing well in a class you're taking? Reflect what you may be telling yourself? This was my problem when I finished my Masters in Business Administration degree. I am not necessarily a logical thinker, so the pursuit of this type of degree was very much a stretch goal. I hate math, finance, and accounting and continually convinced myself that I am not a numbers person. I excelled, however, in theory classes and courses where I could be creative and spontaneous. My negative talk took a toll on me through my program. I failed and repeated my finance class twice and my accounting class three times. Throughout these courses I kept telling myself that I was so challenged in these areas that I had no idea why I was in the program or how I was going to ever graduate. I think that I even used the word "stupid" quite frequently. It was in one of my statistical operations classes that I received a grade better than the top student in the class. When he saw my grade he commented that I was a "brainiac." I cannot begin to explain to you what that comment did for me. I felt that I could achieve the grade I wanted if I worked hard enough and believed in myself. The remainder of my classes were very different. I lost the fear of failure and felt that I had a new level of self-confidence. I only wish someone called me a "brainiac" several years earlier. Never the less, I felt different about myself from that moment on. My lack of self-confidence also prevented me from asking questions in class for fear of looking stupid to the other students. I learned through this experience that everyone has questions and probably the same questions that I had. The only stupid question is the one that does not get asked.

Don't Believe Negative Thoughts

Another critical success factor is to challenge your negative thoughts and do not fall into the trap of believing them. Do you believe everything other people tell you? No. I believe very little of what people tell me without evidence even though I consider myself a very trusting person. That may not be the case with our own self-talk. We have a tendency to believe what we think and not question everything we tell ourselves. After all, it is us, why wouldn't we believe ourselves? We're our own best friend, right? Wrong. Would you say a negative thing to a best friend like you do to yourself? Probably not. So, we need to challenge our negative comments, ourselves and say, "No, this is not true."

In the case of the difficult classes I took, it is not true that I was stupid, even though I thought I was stupid. Maybe my true dislike for math-like subjects prevented me from working as hard as I needed to in the class. I realized that I functioned very differently in the classes I enjoyed and spent the bulk of my study time there. I needed to change my discipline in this area, which I eventually did with great success. I also had to challenge my negative thoughts and actually tell myself these classes were not difficult, I just needed to spend the time and-----------get out of this class. The idea here is not to ignore responsibility with distasteful tasks but rather to learn to maintain diligence and discipline when necessary.

Be Grateful

Another way to improve our positive thought processes is to be ever grateful for what we have and perceive every privilege as a gift. Despite all of the negativity we hear about every day on the news, the world is full of beautiful things to be grateful for. When was the last time you truly looked at the sky or moon? I work very long hours so much of my driving is either at sunset or sunrise. I oftentimes ask people at work if they noticed that great sunrise this morning while they were driving in. I am always surprised when most of them say they didn't even notice it. Beauty is all around us to lift our spirits if we increase our awareness and be thankful for it.

It is also a wonderful practice to be grateful for the people in your life. What would your life be without them? Many of you, who have been challenged with raising children, especially at certain ages, know how frustrating that can be. Whenever I have been frustrated about things my children did, I reflected on how empty my life would be without them and how grateful I am that they are here. Regardless of what is important to you never take the world for granted.

Don't Take Yourself Too Seriously

It is also important to not take yourself too seriously. This is a challenge for many people as it is with me. In reality, when we feel like we are failures, for the most part, no one ever notices. When we make mistakes they oftentimes go unnoticed. We, however, may feel frustrated and demoralized by our mistakes or perceived failures. This is the function of our ego, which is responsible for contributing to our negative thought processes. Not everything is as important as we tend to believe it is. We need to learn to forgive ourselves and move on. It helps to not take yourself too seriously and learn to laugh at some situations rather than feel bad about them. What other people think about us is really a construct of their own mind, a reflection of their own problems and weaknesses, and not a reflection on us. Try not to worry about what others think and try not to take yourself too seriously. Learn to laugh. Learn to take risks, make mistakes and, most importantly, learn from them. As John Wayne said "When you fall off the horse, you need to shake it off and get back on."

Don't Compare Yourself to Others

We are all different from each other, and all of us are destined to contribute something unique to the world we live in. We all are on our own path to achieve what is possible for us. It is our own personal rhythm and the construct of our own values and belief systems, which will move us in the direction of our own achievements.

One problem, however, is the fact that we frequently compare ourselves to others, which invites negativity into our lives and make us feel inferior. We need to move in our personal rhythms, on our own personal plan, and marvel at our own personal successes. We cannot measure our success though comparison of ourselves to the successes of others. This will lead to jealousy, envy and feelings of inferiority. You can use others as role models, mentors, and to help provide direction for us but not as a one on one comparison.

Surround Yourself With Positive People

It is important to make sure that you spend as much time as possible in a positive environment. This includes reducing our exposure to negativity. Have you ever spent time around someone who is chronically negative? What a downer! Negative people can create an environment that is not only difficult but also toxic to live in. Consciously create yourself an environment of positivity by spending more time with positive people. Attitude is contagious!

You can also limit your exposure to negative thoughts by limiting the amount of time you watch programs like the news channel. Have you ever noticed that the news is predominantly negative? Sensationalism is what sells in the media and oftentimes that comes with negativity. Watch the news only to make sure that you are informed, but do not fall into a pattern of chronic viewing. It is also helpful to select movies and reading material that have positive messages. Studies on cancer patients suggest that those people who focused on the creation of a positive environment such as watching comedies, listening to pleasing music and choosing positive friends as support systems do much better through treatment than those who look at the negative side of their situation. So, whenever you can, limit exposure to negativity. Remember when dealing with negative people, you can always walk away.

Be Clear About Your Desires

Once you know what you want out of life, tell those around you. No one can read your mind. The first few chapters of this book have helped to channel your thoughts in this direction so you should have some new insights into what you would like to achieve. Now share them!

Several years ago I did a presentation on healthcare careers to a class of under privileged children in a very poor neighborhood in Detroit. One very nice young lady told a compelling story about her grandmother who was very ill and suffering. She loved her grandmother so much that she wanted to be a nurse but had no money to go to school. There are always programs such as scholarships, financial aid, and loans available, but in this situation, she did not have access to this information. In this case, through my hospital and our local university, we were able to secure grants and scholarships to fund her education if she continued to do well in her studies. The lovely young lady did very well in the program and ended up working for me in one of my critical care departments after she graduated. The only thing that she did was to tell someone about her desires. In this case, she told the right person who could help. There is always support if we look for it.

It also helps to be clear about even the smallest of desires. With all of the hours that I work, at times I come home and look at the work that needs to be done in the house and I feel depressed and overwhelmed. I will go one step further and say that I can easily fall into the trap of feeling sorry for myself if I let that happen. My husband and daughter are always willing to help, but for some reason they don't seem to see what needs to be done the way that I do. When I ask them for help, however, I always get it. So don't be afraid to ask. We all need help from time to time.

Keep Your Energy Level Up

Be positive, positive, positive and more positive. One way to keep positive is to feel good and take care of your body. We will talk at length about this in the next few chapters, but it is important to mention this as a success factor here. Keep your energy up, get enough rest, make a commitment to include renewal activities, and surround yourself with a positive environment.

Let Success Come to You

The last critical success factor is to let success come to you, enjoy it and be grateful for it. Believe it or not, many people are afraid of success.

Directions Affirmation Exercise

The exercise for this chapter will provide you insights into your negative thought rhythms. You probably already have an idea about what you say to yourself, but you probably don't know to what extent you repeat these negative comments. This tool will help give you some insight into the degree of negative self talk that you engage in. You will need to keep this tool handy for one day. Write down your negative statements every time to hear yourself saying them.

At the end of the day, read all of your negative comments and try to understand why you said them to yourself. Do you think that you're stupid because someone in your life has told you that? Do you think that you're fat because you're comparing yourself to someone else, or has someone told you that?

After you think about the origin of your negative thoughts, right next to the negative statement, write a positive affirmation. For instance, if you say to yourself, 'I'm so stupid,' right next to the negative thought, write, 'I am so smart.' If you write, 'I am so fat,' right next to it, write, 'I am at a healthy weight and in control of my life.'

When you complete this exercise, begin to regularly repeat the positive affirmations to yourself several times a day. Carry your list with you and schedule time to read it. Remember that you are now beginning to reprogram your subconscious mind to start making the necessary changes in your behaviors. By doing this, you reprogram your subconscious mind so that your body responds in a way to make you successful.

CHAPTER 6 EXERCISE: NEGATIVE THOUGHTS

	Negative Thoughts/Affirmations
1	
2	
3	
4	
5	
6	
7	
8	
9	
10	
11	
12	
13	
14	
15	
16	
17	
18	
19	
20	
21	
22	
23	
24	
25	
26	
27	
28	
29	
30	
31	
32	
33	
34	

Next Steps

You are well on your way to self-understanding and achieving success. The next four chapters focus on particular topics to improve your health and improve your world. The next chapter will deal with the problems of stress and how we can change our rhythms to manage the challenges of a stressful life.

TAP DANCE INSTRUCTION: OVER THE TOP

The step for this chapter is called over the top because the concepts we have covered in this chapter will take you over the top and transcend you to the next level. This step is done by sliding one foot across the front of the other and jumping over that leg onto the same leg that you use for the liftoff. It is a difficult step, but then life is difficult. You can do this.

CHAPTER 7:
STRESS: WHAT IS IT AND HOW TO CONTROL IT

OBJECTIVES: CHAPTER 7

1. Understand the concept of stress.

2. Understand the effects of stress on the body and your life.

3. Understand your personal stressors.

4. Learn strategies to control stress in your life.

What is Stress?

Very simply, the term stress refers to any demands either physical or emotional placed on the body. Sounds pretty simple when we think of it like that, right? Then why is stress so bad for us? Anything in our life, in small doses, is generally not bad for us including stress. In fact, stress is the body's normal mechanism to kick up our metabolism and energy to meet the body's demands. It readies us for the emotional and physical challenges we face throughout our lives. Some degree of stress is an advantage that peaks our performance by heightening awareness and stimulating the body. For instance, we increase the demand on our body when we exercise. This creates stress on the body. The body responds by increasing heart rate, respiratory rate, speed and power of muscle movement, and mental acuity. The result is the body's ability to meet the demands of the stress and ultimately produce a stronger physique.

The problem with stress is the concern that we, as a society, are under continuous pressure, which keeps us in an overloaded state for protracted periods of time. Busy schedules, multitasking, and environmental pressures all contribute to this phenomenon.

Most people in the United States report that they experience stress on a daily basis. Four out of five people report regular periods of high stress every day. Work stress is reported to have increased by fourfold resulting in stress-related illnesses in the workplace. It is reported that twenty-five percent of all drugs prescribed in the United States are for the treatment of stress and stress-related symptoms, and ninety percent of all illnesses are now attributed to stress, including cardiac disease, hypertension and even cancer.

Categories of Stress

Stress can be classified in two different categories, good (eustress) and bad (distress) stress. Some examples of good stress would be things like getting married, sports events, and new relationships. All of these place stress on your body. The examples of bad stress include things like work pressure, family problems, divorce, and financial challenges. The problem is that regardless of whether the stress is good or bad the body reacts the same way, by invoking the stress response.

If you have ever been married, think back to when you planned your wedding, pretty stressful, right? You were probably feeling pretty fatigued throughout the process and probably were very relieved after the wedding was over. The body cannot determine whether the stress is good versus bad, so the body invokes what is called the stress response to meet the physical and emotional demands placed on it.

The Stress Response

The stress response has been identified as the fight or flight response designed to protect the body by providing a mechanism that supplies immediate energy to the body in times of need. This is accomplished through the secretion of various hormones. There are many stories of Herculean efforts by people in terrible situations where they demonstrated incredible strength and accomplishments. There are even several television shows dedicated to such phenomenon. This tremendous strength and effort is a result of the stress response. The following is a discussion of what happens in the body during the stress response and an algorithm that demonstrates the chain of events.

Stress Response

1. The body perceives a demand called the stressor, which begins the chain of events.

2. This stressor triggers the autonomic nervous system to prepare the body to respond.

3. This causes the secretion of two hormones, adrenalin and cortisol. Adrenalin increases the heart rate, respiratory rate, increases blood pressure, mobilizes energy reserves, increases mental acuity and increases reaction time. Cortisol balances the adrenalin by replenishing the energy supply, improving memory and alerting the immune system.

4. The body responds appropriately to the needs in response to the stress.

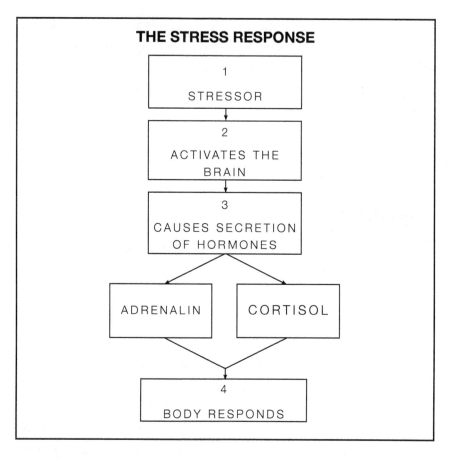

How the Stress Response Works

Let's explore this important concept more closely. Something happens that triggers the stress response in our body. The body perceives that there is an unusual physical or emotional demand on the body that is up and above the normal activity state. This we call the stressor. The stressor then activates the brain, which responds by doing two things. It first triggers the automatic nervous system. If you place your hand on a hot stove, before you even feel the heat, your body reacts and pulls back the hand to prevent injury. This happens automatically and in a split second time frame. This is the automatic nervous system. If your body waited long enough for you to realize what is happening and feel the heat, you would be burned.

If you are driving down the freeway and someone cuts you off, you react by either slamming on the breaks or swerving to avoid an accident. You don't stop and think, 'oh my, this person is cutting me off. I need to turn right to get around them then turn back to get my car back on the road.' You automatically invoke the stress response and swerve around to prevent an accident. When you realize what just happened you probably feel shaky or stressed. This is the autonomic nervous system reacting to prevent injury.

When the brain becomes activated, the body secretes two hormones, adrenaline and cortisol, which work together to accomplish the stress response. Adrenaline increases your heart rate, respiratory rate, blood pressure, and helps metabolize the energy reserves necessary for the stress response. Adrenaline also increases your mental acuity and increases your reaction time so the body can move very quickly.

Cortisol, on the other hand, works together with adrenaline, but its role is to balance the adrenaline by replenishing energy supplies, improving memory, and boosting the immune system. This helps to provide long-term protection and recovery for the body following the event. The goal of the stress response is to help your body survive. Every stressor that you encounter invokes the stress response. The degree of the response depends on the perceived magnitude of the event.

Think about a time when you had to do something that was stressful to you. An example would be public speaking or a challenging meeting with your boss. How do you feel? You may get butterflies, or you may actually feel ill. Your heart rate goes up, your respiratory rate goes up, and your blood pressure is high. You are preparing to meet the demands of the event. This physiological reaction places stress on the body to provide optimal performance. Negative effects on the body can become apparent when the stress response becomes prolonged or repetitive. The body needs time to rest and recover, and this level of stress does not allow for that time. In the long run, prolonged exposure to stress can result in serious changes in the body.

External Stressors

Everybody experiences stress from two major categories of input, external or internal sources. External sources are those that come from the environment around us. Internal sources are those that come from our mental thought processing. Here are examples of both.

External factor stressors that come from the environment are usually unpredicted events. Car accidents, weather and storm tragedies, sudden injury, or sudden death of a loved one are all unpredicted events. In the past few years, we have had terrible experiences with storms such as Hurricane Katrina. The tragedy of 9/11 is another unprecedented example.

The external world presents stress for us as well. Globalization is creating pressures in industry resulting in increased work stress. War and global unrest are also examples of external-environmental stress that we live with on a daily basis. Our own work environment is also an external cause of stress for us and has been identified as one of the major causes of external stress in the USA.

Family situations that cause stress are also external forces. The incidence of abuse across the country continues to increase which is a tremendous source of stress for those experiencing this reality. Living in less than optimal situations at home is another example of external stressors that can result in disastrous experiences for those in this type of environment. These situations also provide continual stress whereby the family members may not have the ability to escape to allow for periods of rest and reprieve.

Internal Stressors

Internal sources of stress are related to our own personal beliefs and perceptions of stress, as well as a personal choice for behaviors that place us in a stressful situation. Being aware of the internal stressors is the first step in learning to manage them.

Personal Behaviors

Personal behaviors are internal sources that can create high degrees of stress. Addictive behaviors create stress in many different ways. For instance, substance abuse, whether it is alcohol or drugs, clouds our perception of reality and causes changes in behaviors that can result in situations that create stress. Over time, addictive behaviors can lead to loss of relationships, loss of a job or career, and destruction of health, all of which increase the level of stress.

Dangerous Health Habits

Dangerous health habits are also internal sources of stress, which affect not only the individual suffering through the challenges but also the family. Many diseases are a result of over eating, smoking, and lack of exercise. These can be a direct result of poor personal choices. Disease inflicts a tremendous amount of stress on the body.

Fatigue

Another internal stressor is that of fatigue especially in the context of how much you do through the course of your day and how tired you are. Many of us don't realize that the effect of prolonged fatigue on the body increases stress and increases the potential for disease. We will be discussing this when we talk about the importance of sleep later in the book.

Personal Perceptions

One of our greatest challenges with the management of stress is the control over our own minds and our personal perceptions. Perceptions are our own reality and not necessarily truth, yet we oftentimes accept them as true. These perceptions therefore create unrealistic fears, which increase our stress. Almost all of these fears are unrealized, yet we allow them to negatively affect us and increase our stress levels. Analysis of our fears, in many cases, will reveal that the origin of many of our fears relate to our egos, the fear of looking bad to others, or being perceived as unsuccessful.

"If you were distressed by anything external,
the pain is not due to the thing itself, but to your estimation of it.
And this you have the power to revoke at every moment."
—Marcus Aurelius.

Many of our fears are about being out of control. Few events are stressful in themselves. I'll give you an example. What about driving in rush hour traffic? The event of driving through rush hour traffic in and of itself is not necessarily stressful. We all manage to somehow get through it on a daily basis. So what if we get to our destination a little later. For many of us, traffic can turn into an incredibly stressful situation. Road rage has increased exponentially over time resulting in accidents and injury. We have created this internal stress in our own minds. The reality is that we cannot move traffic any faster and don't have any control over the situation, so why worry about it? This is an example of a time when we need to relinquish the desire to control the environment and roll with the situation.

The notion of relinquishing control has always been a personal challenge for me. Early on in my leadership career I felt the need to control every situation and person with whom I worked. This need for control always resulted in tremendous stress and feelings of failure. Once I learned to relinquish control, my stress level dropped and my life became easier.

A dear friend of mine would always put life back into perspective for me through her consistent words of advice, which were simply, "It is what it is." For some reason, this phrase made perfect sense to me, and I learned to realize that I had control over one thing and one thing only, my mind, reflected in my own attitude and personal reaction to the event. I realized that I could choose to worry about it, or I could choose to let it go. This simple realization proved to be very liberating to me since now I felt in control of the ability to react or to let go.

Scarlet O'Hara in *Gone with the Wind* taught me a couple pearls of wisdom that I use in my daily life to combat fears and stress. Her first saying is, "I will think about that tomorrow." I have found that if I give myself permission to ponder a situation and put it on the back burner for a while, I make better decisions and feel less stressed. It is not about running away from fears and stressors or procrastinating, but rather giving yourself time to react in a constructive way. Scarlet's other great line that I use with great regularity is, "Tomorrow is another day." This type of thinking can give you mini vacations from your stress to help you regroup and recover, as well as provide hope.

We all have particular stressors that present challenges for us. For me, I still hate getting on an airplane. No matter how much I fly, I have not been able to conquer this fear. When I analyze why I feel this way, it is because it represents the ultimate in being out of control. If we realize our particular challenges, however, we can plan for them and develop a process to deal with them.

Physical Effects of Stress

Reflect for a moment on what we discussed in the last chapter about our thoughts as energy. All of our thoughts and feelings such as fear, anxiety, hatred, anger, and jealousy affect our body and can ultimately have a negative effect on our health. These feelings create stress in our lives through alteration of several physiological processes.

Immune System

One very important concern is the fact that prolonged stress decreases the strength of the body's immune system. This happens through a decrease in the activity of both the T-cells and NK-cells. The T-cells are those that protect us from infections or invading organisms such as colds and the flu. The NK-cells are the natural killer cells in the body that are responsible for the elimination of abnormal cells connected to the growth of cancers. Research supports that prolonged periods of high stress can cause diseases such as cancer.

Hormone Secretion

Stress invokes the stress response that we discussed previously. There is an increase in the secretion of the flight hormone adrenaline, which increases the body's stress level. This increases the blood pressure, heart rate, respiratory rate, and reaction time. Prolonged periods of high stress hormones do not allow for the body to rest and recuperate.

Disease States

Over time prolonged stress can lead to diseases such as hypertension, cardiac disease, type II diabetes, and cancer. Stress can also cause muscular aches especially in the back and neck. Tension or migraine headaches can also be side effects of stress. Stomach problems such as cramping, diarrhea, ulcers, heartburn, eating disorders, and irritable bowel syndrome may be secondary to stress. Weight gain or weight loss may be a problem depending how individuals react to stress. Stress can also result in hair loss, irregular heartbeat or palpitations, as well as triggering asthma attacks, shortness of breath, chest pain, sweating, sweating hands and feet, or cold hands. You have probably noticed skin breakouts during stressful times, and in extreme cases, fertility and the ability to reproduce can be hindered. It has also been identified that children under tremendous stress in the home will actually experience growth and mental development problems.

Emotional Side Effects

There are also emotional symptoms of stress that can be very serious. Things like anxiety, nervousness, anxiety attacks, depression, mood swings, and irritable personality can lead to anger and violence. We have all heard of and may have been victims of road rage secondary to stress. Memory loss, inability to concentrate, feelings of being out of control, substance abuse, and phobias are prevalent in high stress situations. There has been some research about what is termed "withdrawal activities" in cases of stress. Withdrawal activities are exactly that, individuals feel that they need to withdraw from society. Some of these withdrawal activities include calling in sick to work, withdrawing from family and friends, staying home, not engaging in healthy activities, and increased sleep. Post-traumatic stress syndrome is a serious side effect of stress and in the worse cases, suicide.

Directions: Evaluate Your Stress

Your exercise for this chapter is to identify your stressors. Keep this tool with you for one day and identify any incident that you think increases your stress level. Whenever you experience any stress, write it on this tool including the date and time, the situation and what was the stressor. Place a check in the box to identify whether the stressor came from either the environment or from a mental, internal source. For instance, if you are driving down the freeway and someone cuts you off, that would be an environmental stress. If you are doing a presentation and are nervous about it, that would be internal stress. Lastly, if you have been placed in physical danger check that since these will be stressors that you may not be able to control. There is also a comment section for you to capture your thoughts or feelings.

CHAPTER 7 EXERCISE: IDENTIFICATION OF STRESS

Identify Your Stressors

Date	Time	Situation	What was the stressor / why	Where were you	Physical danger Yes/No	Comments

CHAPTER 7 EXERCISE: IDENTIFICATION OF STRESS

Identify Your Stressors

Date	Time	Situation	What was the stressor / why	Where were you	Physical danger Yes/No	Comments

Once you are finished filling out your stress log, review your document and identify how many of the stressors did not result in an adverse situation. It is probably the majority of them. This will help you put your day into perspective and identify where you can control your stress by changing your attitude toward certain events. In cases of serious illness, this tool will not apply since you may be dealing with life or death situations that are inherently stressful.

Meditation Moment (MM)

Once you have identified what routinely makes you stressed, you can learn to control your reactions. I use what I call my meditation moment or MM. This technique helps you to take a quick time-out to review your stress and develop a quick strategy to handle it. This process takes just a couple seconds and has three distinct steps. These steps provide a logical analysis and strategy to deal with your stress. The steps are to assess, analyze, and reason. You first need to recognize your stressor and then ask yourself four quick questions. What just happened? What was the stressor? Why is it bothering me? And, how can I adapt my attitude? Once the meditation moment becomes a natural rhythm to you, you'll be able to control your body's response to stress through a systematic process.

Let's use the traffic example. What just happened? I'm frustrated because I am stuck in a traffic jam. What is the stressor? I will be late for work. Why is it bothering me? I don't want to look bad to my boss. How can I adapt my attitude? By realizing that I have no control over this situation, I will make a cell phone call to let someone at work know my dilemma.

Next Steps

By now you have a great understanding of who you are, why you are, what your goals are, and what your particular challenges are in regards to positive thinking and stress. The next three chapters are focused on creating rhythms of personal behavior to help you stay healthy and move toward success.

TAP DANCE INSTRUCTION: NERVE TAP

The nerve tap is a perfect step to learn following our discussion of stress. Here is how you do it. Stand on one leg and extend your other leg to the side. Repeatedly tap your toe on the floor as fast as you can while keeping your toes very low to the ground.

CHAPTER 8:
THE RHYTHM OF EXERCISE: ITS MAGIC EFFECTS ON YOUR HEALTH

OBJECTIVES: CHAPTER 8

1. Learn about the benefits of exercise

2. Learn the different types of exercise

3. Learn how to exercise safely

4. Learn the success factors to keep you exercising

Now that you understand your own personal rhythms and how they affect your life, the next step is to learn strategies to stay healthy. The focus of these next three chapters is on what I call the "Trifecta of health," or three vital behavioral rhythms necessary for optimal health. They are exercise, sleep, and good nutrition. The research about the importance of exercise to health is irrefutable. Study after study links exercise to positive outcomes and healthy, happy lives; yet only a small percentage of the population engages in regular physical activity. Even in the elderly, exercise programs started as late seventies, eighties, and nineties have yielded phenomenal results with improved strength and overall improved quality of life.

An example of the value of exercise can be found in the exercise icon Jack LaLanne. I had the wonderful opportunity to do a presentation at a health and wellness conference with him several years ago in Arkansas.

At that time he was in his late eighties, but he looked and behaved like someone in his late forties or early fifties. After lecturing all day, the group of us would go out to dinner and afterwards, dancing. I was tired, but Jack wasn't. He truly is an example of living your values and developing healthy rhythms. His diet rhythms are amazing. His exercise rhythms are amazing. He has never smoked. He doesn't drink. He gets enough rest. He has always been an inspiration to me! Spending time with someone this balanced and phenomenal was truly a gift I will always treasure and living proof of how important it is to take care of your health.

Advantages of Exercise

There are so many advantages to exercise that it is a wonder why so many of us do not make the time to fit exercise into our lives. Here are just some of them:

- Improves our physical strength

- Strengthens the immune system

- Improves the cardiovascular system

- Improves the function of the digestive system

- It decreases fat stores

- It increases metabolism

- Improves flexibility

- Improves balance, especially as we age

- Increases physical endurance

- Restores our personal control

- It decreases stress

- Improves self-esteem

- Decreases the risk of diabetes, especially Type-II

- Improves brain function including coordination and memory

- Decreases risk of stroke

- Decreases the risk of cancer

- Decreases the incidence of osteoporosis

- Reduces blood pressure

- Decreases incidence of heart disease

- Improves mental health

- Improves coordination and motor function

- Promotes restful sleep

- Provides a social outlet

- Improves the respiratory system

- Decreases incidence of colds and flu.

Now, if there was a pill that did that all for you wouldn't you buy it? Of course you would!

How Much Exercise Do We Need?

There has always been a debate about how much exercise we need to be healthy. The answer is, not as much as you think. To maintain your health, the Surgeon General recommends thirty to sixty minutes of daily physical activity. Don't believe the media hype of no pain, no gain. At times, the pain we experience is what prevents us from exercising. The simple goal of exercise is to overload the body just enough to force the body to respond by becoming stronger and more fit. That is not to the point of pain. For instance, I want to begin a walking program so I start very slowly. The first week I do ten minutes a day, the next week I do fifteen minutes a day, and overtime, the sessions become longer and I progressively overload the body. When beginning a weight-training program perhaps you can lift five pounds, the muscles start to respond and become stronger so it is necessary to increase the weight to eight pounds then ten or more. Once again, this demonstrates the principal of overload.

Exercise does not need to take place all at one time either. This activity can be cumulative throughout the day. You can exercise for fifteen minutes in the morning and fifteen minutes in the afternoon, or you can do the entire thirty minutes in one session. If you think about breaking up your exercise sessions, it may become more manageable to work exercise into a busy schedule. Many organizations have walking programs at lunch, or maybe you walk your dog a couple of times a day. All of this contributes to your cumulative physical activity and burns more calories over time.

Aerobic Exercise

Aerobic exercise is any activity that stresses the cardiovascular system for a prolonged period of time. In order to burn fat, the body needs enough oxygen. This is achieved through activities that increase the heart rate and respiratory rate. You have probably heard about being in the target zone and monitoring your heart rate to ensure that you are at the level where you are burning fat. Let's make that a little simpler. Exercise at a level where you feel the activity feels somewhat hard. You should never feel that you are working to the point of excessive fatigue or that you cannot talk through your work out. In other words, exercise for fifteen to forty minute sessions at moderate intensity three to five times a week.

Any activity that raises the heart and respiratory rate for a prolonged period of time can be considered aerobic activities. These would be activities like walking, jogging, swimming, group fitness classes or any type of aerobic equipment like a bike, trekker, or treadmill. You will also be more successful with your exercise program if you choose activities that you enjoy.

Resistance Training

Resistance training is also very important to our physical fitness. Aerobic activity strengthens the cardiovascular system, but resistance training targets the muscles, joints and structures to improve overall strength. Resistance training also helps to contour the body to help you see the results you are looking for. I have heard from many of my clients that when they do only aerobics they loose their fat but seem to remain flabby. In their mind, they are a thinner version of their heavier selves. Building muscle tissue can actually change the look and proportions of the body.

Another benefit of resistance training that you may not realize is the increase in lean muscle mass. Muscles become bigger and denser. The muscle cells require more energy and therefore, the larger the muscles, the more calories you will burn at rest. Every pound of muscle mass burns approximately fifty calories at rest per day. Your metabolic rate goes up when you build muscle, which helps you burn more calories and ultimately lose fatter.

Working with weights is also important to improve and maintain strength. Especially as we become older, this strength helps us maintain our mobility and perform activities of daily living with far more efficiency and longer into our lives. This added muscle mass also helps to prevent injury especially in the case of a fall. Bone strength also improves with the pressure to the bones and joints to prevent, or decrease, the progression of osteoporosis. Resistance training begun with senior citizens in their seventies, and nineties has shown great improvement in physical functioning and mobility. Falls that result in fractures and severe injury are frequent causes of death and debilitation in the elderly.

For resistance training to be effective, you need to work all of the muscles of the body twice a week. This gives the body a chance to heal and respond in between workouts so that the muscles can grow and adapt to the stress. You can train all of your muscles at one time in a circuit-like program twice week, or you can break up your workouts over several days a week. For instance, on Monday, you may want to do your upper body. On Tuesday, you do your lower body. On Wednesday, you repeat upper body, and Thursday, you repeat your lower body. With limited time, or if you are looking for more rapid or specific results, you can train chest, shoulder and triceps one day, back and biceps another day, and legs the third day. Take a day off between the three days and begin the series again. You have a great deal of flexibility in your program.

As you begin your resistance-training program, it may be helpful for you to seek the advice of a personal trainer. Or, purchase a book on weight training to make sure that you are selecting the appropriate exercises and performing them with the appropriate form. You also want to prevent injury and achieve results as soon as possible. A certified trainer will be able to target your program to your particular goals and monitor your success.

Mind/Body/Spirit Exercises

The mind, body, and spirit exercises are another type of activity that is receiving a great deal of positive press lately and is very good for the body. These are activities such as yoga, Pilates, Tai Chi and a whole genre of exercises that incorporate the mind and spirit in a holistic approach to strengthening the body and enhancing awareness of the spirit. Specific advantages to these forms of exercise include heightened mental awareness and personal control, improved flexibility, strength, and balance. Relaxation and peace are tremendous advantages to these types of exercises that also can help reduce stress and provide a sense of well-being. These exercise forms also incorporate the use of the breath for control and focus, which provides a healthy oxygen level for healing the body.

It may be helpful for you to do some research on the various forms of mind-body exercise and to take several classes to find the program that interests you the most. For instance, there are several different types of yoga classes. Prior to judging yoga as a choice of exercise for you, experiment with the different types of yoga before you make your choice as to what feels best for you.

Stretching

Stretching in of itself, can be considered a form of exercise and is becoming more important in the prevention of injuries and maintenance of flexibility over time. Anyone who exercises regularly should do a light stretch in the beginning of the session that is targeted to rehearsal of movement and increased range of motion. Following the activity, the stretch should be prolonged and held for fifteen to thirty seconds to increase the range of motion and prevent tightening of the joints and muscles. All muscles that have been used should be the targets of the stretches. Stretching is also important in rehabilitation of injuries and in improving mobility in the elderly. As we age, without exercise and stretching, mobility of the joints is lost over time.

Rhythm Success Factors

There are several success factors to incorporate into your exercise program to help you be successful. It is important to make sure your efforts are rewarded with results. Over my years as a personal trainer, I have heard so many people complain that they exercise all the time yet they don't see results. These success factors can help you see progress and achieve your desired outcomes.

Listen to Your Body

First of all, listen to your body because the way you feel changes from day to day. Your body's performance ability will also change from day to day. This is a result of many factors including your diet, how much rest you have had, stressors in your life, the amount of water you drink and whether you are battling some type of infection or disease. You may also have an injury or muscular soreness that could affect your exercise program. Whatever the reason, it is important to be aware of your body's condition at any time and adjust your exercise type and intensity to compensate. My rule of thumb is, if it doesn't feel right, or if it hurts, don't do it. It is also not recommended to exercise when you feel that you are coming down with the cold or flu. If you have a temperature, fever, sore throat, or general feelings of illness, you should rest. If you feel especially fatigued, or if your muscles are already sore from a past workout, then, listen to your body and give it a chance to rest. Your body is telling you that at this time, it cannot manage all of the stress and needs some recovery.

Education

Understanding what you are doing, why you are doing it, and how to do it correctly are very important in regards to exercise. You may decide it is time to get in shape so you go into a gym, start jumping around in a class, maybe you wander to the weights and do a few moves out there, but you may not necessarily know what you are doing or how to make your program effective. Many people leave exercise programs because they don't see the results they want to see, and that may be because they don't understand what they need to do or don't know how to choose the right exercises. Personal trainers can help you design a program based on sound principles of fitness, which include the factors of intensity, duration and frequency all necessary to build an effective and comprehensive exercise program. These three factors need to be aligned appropriately in order to see results from an exercise program.

You can improve the chances of success with your program if you seek information. This can be done by your own personal research on the Internet or by purchasing exercise books and publications. This can more easily be achieved by finding a good certified personal trainer to help create and guide your program. You may choose to work with a personal trainer for a short time until you learn what you need to know to create your own programs, or you can stay with a personal trainer to help you with motivation and specific results. If you are going to take group fitness classes, make sure that all of the instructors are certified.

Realistic Role Models

Selecting role models can be very helpful throughout our lives no matter what we want to learn or achieve. The problem is selecting the right role model to motivate and teach you the right things. The same should be true for fitness. It is not uncommon for us to look at someone and say we want to be just like him or her. The fact that we want to look just like those we see in the ads or on the product cover or in the book is what sells exercise and fitness products. We need to realize that fitness stars exercise for a living. It is natural for someone who exercises to that extent to remain physically fit. We need to be realistic with ourselves and take into consideration our personal commitments such as jobs; family, and personal time limitations that will prevent us from spending adequate time towards this goal.

You want to select a realistic role model, or someone you know who works similar hours as you do, has personal challenges in their life and yet continues to make a commitment to themselves in regards to their health and fitness rhythms. For me, I identify with individuals at work or with people I meet in my gym who manages this very well. It is then easy to say, if they can do it, I can do it. Realistically, you will never be like someone who has completely different rhythms from yours.

Appropriate Program Selection

A very important factor to successful exercising is appropriate program selection. You need to choose an activity that you enjoy and will continue to do. For instance, jogging and running have always bothered my knees, so no matter how many times I have tried to include this as an exercise in my program, I can't. I substitute running and jogging with walking, biking or group exercise classes of a low impact variety. I love to be out in nature, so my summer activities include kayaking, biking, and hiking. Because I love all of these activities, I will keep them in my schedule and actually look forward to them.

There are several types of group exercise activities that you can find in any fitness center which range from body sculpting to kick boxing or step classes. My recommendation is to select the classes that sound interesting to you. Begin by reading the description of the class, and then take test classes to see which ones you enjoy. I have had many people over the years say that they do not enjoy aerobic classes because of an experience they had in one class. That may only be true for that one class possibly due to the class format or instructor.

Instructors are critical to successful group fitness class experience. A good instructor will be certified and interested in your progress in the class and not there for their own fitness goals. The class should be taught in a multilevel format to accommodate the needs of all exercisers unless the class is particularly billed as high level or high intensity. This means that the instructor will demonstrate the average intensity level and provide examples of how to increase or decrease the activity to meet personal fitness levels. All classes can be adjusted this way if the instructor is skilled at teaching.

The selection of appropriate exercise equipment will also help you to stay with a program. Whether you are looking for equipment at the gym or something for home, try several types of equipment before you decide. At the gym, you can vary your workouts on treadmills, stair climbers, stationary bikes, or trekkers all of which provide aerobic activity in different ways. Do what feels best for you. If you are selecting something for your home, pick your favorite activity since this will be your only option. Appropriate program selection will keep you enjoying your program for a longer period of time.

Support Systems

I always recommend the identification of a support system to help keep you on track with your goals. A family member can provide this to you by either supporting you emotionally or helping you with chores or tasks, so you can free up necessary time for yourself. I hear so often that women feel bad asking their husbands to "baby sit," so they can go work out. First of all, we need to lose the term "baby sitting" and realize that this is parenting and a part of their inherent responsibility. It may be helpful to create a schedule that seems fair for everyone so that all personal needs will be met and everyone can equally enjoy activities. In our house, I love to exercise and dance, and my husband loves to fish. He goes away on his weekends with the guys, and I take time during the week to work out. This works for us, but maybe you and your spouse could get in shape together and convert this into quality time for both of you. In my experience, I have a good friend and the two of us always seem to be on opposite mood schedules for exercise. This actually works great. When she is not in the mood to exercise, I am, and when I'm not in the mood to exercise, she is. We can intimidate each other until we go exercising together, which works out to both of our advantages. It also helps that we are both fitness instructors and enjoy the same outdoor activities.

A support system could also be your dog. You can take your dog for a walk and incorporate an exercise program around this activity. The exercise will benefit both of you and result in better fitness for you and your pet.

Set Realistic Goals

In our chapter on goal setting we discussed this as an important factor for the achievement of any goal. The same is true in our exercise and fitness goals. As a trainer, I have had clients coming to me saying that their goal was to lose thirty pounds in a short time to fit into a dress or to look good at their class reunion. These are not realistic goals, and there is no way to be successful. You will always set yourself up for failure. Set goals that are achievable. Losing weight at one to two pounds per week is probably about as achievable and safe as we can get.

Reward Yourself

In the past, we talked quite a bit about rewarding yourself. Apply those rewards to your exercise goals and plan on doing something nice for yourself when you achieve certain milestones in your program. Maybe you want to buy yourself something small for every five pounds you lose and then buy yourself something wonderful when you reach your goal weight. Don't ever reward yourself with food! This is counterproductive to what you have just worked so hard to achieve. I have had people say to me that they are going to sit down with a whole gallon of ice cream when they lose their weight because then they wouldn't feel guilty eating it. This does not even make sense to me---I hope it does not make sense to you either.

Mix it Up

Variety is the spice of life, but we are creatures of habit and easily fall into a rut. This also applies to your exercise programs. The same exercise routine over and over can become boring and a chore instead of an enjoyable activity. It is important for you to also train in a way that the muscles are always challenged and in balance. The same activity over and over will not produce a balanced, strong body especially if you are targeting only specific muscle groups. Mixing it up will take care of both of these concerns. Mix up your classes, mix up your weight program, and vary your activities during summer and winter months. Do things differently, make it new!

Measure Your Improvement

When you see results, you become motivated so measure your results from exercise. I don't recommend that you become a slave to your scale, which can be demoralizing. When you exercise, your muscles become denser and therefore heavier, your bones also become stronger and heavier, so initially you may not see a great reduction in your weight. Weight, in of itself, is not an indication of health. In fact, athletes can be heavy and yet have very little body fat. It is the percent of body fat that you need to monitor. You can do this a couple of ways. If you have a personal trainer, they can test your body fat periodically to see how you are progressing. I happen to like to use a less technical and less expensive way of measuring body fat and that is looking in the mirror. See if you are losing fat by what you look like. Also, pay attention to how your clothes are fitting. Can you get into some of those old clothes that you no longer wear? You are then losing fat.

Schedule Your Activity

Once you commit to exercising, get it in your daily schedule. This will allow you to arrange your activities around the inclusion of exercise. It can be at different times throughout the week, and it can be different activities. For instance, if you drop the kids off at dance or soccer, schedule some time to walk or run to a gym for the time the kids will be busy. If you walk the dog when you get home, increase the time and make that a more intense workout; schedule activities on weekends. At times you will need to be flexible, and we all know that there are times that schedules self-destruct for various reasons. However, you will have a better chance of meeting your goal of exercise if you schedule it.

Exercising Safely

As with much of what we do in life, exercise has some risks and there are important guidelines for exercising safely. Many of the fitness organizations agree that once an individual has reached the age of fifty for women and over the age of forty for men, it is recommended to seek the advice of a physician who may decide that you need an exercise stress test prior to beginning an exercise program. Also, anyone with some type of pre-existing disease such as heart disease or diabetes should talk to his or her physician before starting a program.

It is safe to exercise if you have physical challenges. The key, however, to exercising safely with physical challenges is the selection of a unique approach to exercise based on your physical needs. Pregnancy is a good example. It's always been said that if you're pregnant, you should not start an exercise program. However, if you've been exercising before you were pregnant it is safe to exercise as long as you modify your program to meet the needs of your changing body. This is best done in collaboration with your physician.

We already spoke about getting to know the needs of the body and the importance of modifying the activity to prevent injury or pain. This is important regardless of whether you have physical challenges or not, but it is extremely important in the presence of disease. If you are exercising with cardiac disease be aware of the signs and symptoms of heart attacks that can always be a risk with increased stress on the body. Any feelings of tightness or pain in the chest in this situation are reasons to stop and seek help. In the case of diabetes, dizziness, weakness, profuse sweating, or loss of coordination could be signs of low blood sugar. You need to stop, test your sugar and drink some juice if necessary.

Especially if you are beginning an exercise program, take it slow. You've heard of the weekend warriors that work all week and on a weekend are out there playing sports or catching up in the gym. On Monday, they feel sore and tired or have suffered an injury. It is better to exercise twice a week on the weekends than not at all, just take it slow and listen to your body. Start with fifteen minutes of exercise a day then increase to twenty, twenty-five, thirty or more minutes progressively. Fitness is a journey where we continually strive to get stronger and feel better. There is nothing that says that you have to go from zero to sixty minutes. So, take some time and work up to your desired intensity.

There are a couple other thoughts for you to remember. Most importantly, never give up and never surrender, and keep moving towards your goal. Be positive and remember that you are human. Think about how long it took you to get out of shape. We start in pretty good shape whey we were young. Over time, without attention to exercise and diet, we slowly gained our weight over many, many years. It is realistic to believe that we need to slowly lose our weight as well.

Directions: Evaluate your Exercise Rhythms

You don't have a new tool for this chapter because you already evaluated your exercise rhythms in chapter one. For this chapter, go back to your first tool and review your section on exercise to analyze your pattern. For those of you who don't exercise, this will be easy because there will not be anything there. Review your weekly log and see where you could fit in some exercise. If you watch a lot of TV, maybe you could carve out some time from that activity for exercise. You could even put a recumbent bike in front of the TV and exercise while you watch. Initially, include exercise in some form three times a week and attempt this for a month. After a month, increase to four and then five sessions a week at times that you can realistically fit exercise into your schedule. Make the commitment to exercise even if it is marching in front of your TV for thirty minutes.

Formally schedule the activity, and in a month or so, evaluate how you feel. You will feel stronger, you will have seen some change in your body, and you will feel more in control of your life. I have found while working with people in fitness programs that the signs of success are what becomes the motivating factor to continue—you just need to start!

Next Steps

Now that you are aware of your exercise rhythms and have some ideas how to change them, we can move on to our next topic in the Trifecta of health, which is the science of sleep.

TAP DANCE INSTRUCTION: SHUFFLE HOP

Your next tap step is called the shuffle hop and is very aerobic if you repeat it. You perform this step by brushing your foot out, brushing it back in, hopping on that foot while transferring your weight from side to side. Repeat it while alternating and shifting weight.

CHAPTER 9:
ALL ABOUT SLEEP RHYTHMS

OBJECTIVES: CHAPTER 9

1. Learn about sleep

2. Learn the importance of sleep in our lives

3. Learn strategies to improve the quality of sleep

Status of Sleep in the U.S.

The second component of the Trifecta of health is sleep. Sleep is extremely vital to our overall health and personal success; yet sleep is usually not included in the discussions or ranked at the same level of importance as exercise and nutrition. Hopefully, this chapter will enlighten you as to how important healthy sleep rhythms are in your life. Insufficient sleep affects us as a society, and the status of sleep in the United States is not very good.

We live in a crazy, busy society and we are all right in the middle of endless activity. We try to pack so much into our days that usually the easiest thing to sacrifice in our day is sleep. Think back to the last time you were so tired that all you wanted to do was sleep. This happens quite frequently to me, and I would bet that this happens quite frequently to you. Statistics show us that fifty percent of our population is sleep-deprived on a regular basis. There are several reasons for this, including longer work schedules, longer commutes to and from work, increased activities of children, eldercare, and regardless of the reason, as a result we become sleep deprived.

These are frightening statistics and important to realize that many tragedies have been linked to sleep deprivation, including the Exxon-Valdez oil spill and the Chernobyl nuclear event. Evidence found that these two events were directly related to sleep deprivation of the individuals left in charge. Automobile accidents average about 100,000 a year that are directly related to lack of sleep. Employers report decrease in productivity due to sleep deprivation in their employees. Road rage and violence increase in situations of heightened irritability, secondary to sleep deprivation. About one third of all drivers will fall asleep or doze off behind the wheel of a car during the course of their driving life. You may have done that in the past. I know I have had times where I have been so tired that I may have dozed off for a second and needed to look up at a freeway sign because I had lost track of where I was.

Lack of sleep decreases your stress threshold and increases your stress response. It is not only the reduced number of hours of sleep, which are of concern, but it is also a lack of sleep secondary to insomnia and sleep disorders that are prevalent in our society. The problem of sleep deprivation has resulted in an evolving field of medicine recognized by the American Medical Association as sleep medicine. This field focuses on the diagnostic reasons for sleep disorders and the necessary methods of treatment of these sleep disorders. Regardless of the reason for sleep deprivation, the result is always the same, a society that is facing challenges due to a generalized reduction of sleep.

What Is Sleep?

So what is sleep? Can sleep simply be defined as a resting state for both the physical body as well as the mind? The body and mind rests secondary to the blockage of most external stimuli. What is interesting, however, is that the brain itself never rests. In fact, it is just as active during sleep as it is during our wakeful time. Researchers still have not determined why we sleep if the brain doesn't.

There are two major theories that have been proposed. These include the need for restorative sleep, which makes us restore our bodies and replace what we have lost through the day and the theory of adaptive sleep.

Restorative Sleep

Restorative sleep is exactly that, a chance for the body to restore itself. Sleep allows the body and mind to restore itself and reenergize for the next day's activities. Have you ever felt extremely tired when you were ill? That is the result of the body's need to rest and repair. When you are sick, sometimes all you can do is sleep. During restorative sleep, the brain performs cleanup work at night by processing information received through the day and organizing your thoughts, feelings and your memories. The brain tissue and the nerve cells are also repaired during this time. The rest of the body also has a chance to restore itself at night by repairing damage to muscles, joints, and organs. In fact, if you exercise, it is recommended that you get an extra hour of sleep for every hour of exercise to allow the body to restore itself after the stress on your muscles and joints.

Growth hormone is secreted in greater amounts during sleep, which is responsible for the growth of children and the repair of muscles and joints in adults. The immune system also gets a tremendous boost at night when it has a chance to rest.

Adaptive Sleep

The adaptive theory of sleep supports the notion that human beings were designed for hunting and gathering during the day hours, leading to the need for rest at night. This relates to our earlier discussions of Circadian rhythm. Human beings are designed for daytime activities. Our sight and visual acuity do not provide for evening activities. The adaptive theory of sleep supports the need to sleep during the dark hours since nothing else could be accomplished at this time and be ready for necessary activities during the day.

Physiology of Sleep

The physiology of sleep is very complex, so we will not go into the depth of the theory but rather provide a basic overview. This will help explain what goes on during sleep.

As mentioned in the adaptive theory of sleep, our brain functions within our Circadian rhythm. When it's dark, we want to sleep, and when it's light, we want to be awake. The reason for this rhythm is the activity of the structures in the brain, which are called the suprachiasmatic nuclei or SCN. These SCNs are very sensitive to light and responsible for the alternating of sleep and wakeful periods. It is common for people to experience sleepy periods during the day, about every twelve hours. These will be usually mid-afternoon and then late in the evening. Ever experience a two o'clock meeting where you could hardly keep your eyes open? This sleepiness represents our need for periodic rest. Some cultures respond to this need by allowing for rest periods during the day such as siestas. In the United States, we ignore the need to rest and push our bodies late into the night.

Sleep Cycles

There are two basic sleep states: the non-REM and the REM sleep. These sleep cycles alternate through the night in ninety to one-hundred and ten-minute cycles. In the case of optimal sleep, the body will cycle through these cycles about four to five times a night. That is one reason why uninterrupted sleep is so important. Allowing for this cycling can fulfill your body's need for rest and mental processing. Your non-REM sleep cycle is what happens before sleep and constitutes about seventy-five percent of total sleep. It's categorized into four distinct stages that range from dozing to deep sleep.

Stage 1. Dozing: At this point, sleep is very light and the person is easily aroused. This is when you are lying in bed, the lights are out, and you are starting to doze off. Your eyes are closing, but you remain aware of your surroundings. If you hear a noise, you are still alert enough to be able to function and respond quickly.

Stage 2: This is the beginning of sleep, and on your way to deepening levels of unconsciousness. You are still relatively easy to arouse at this point but are less responsive to the world around you. Sometimes you may experience the feeling of falling, which causes your body to jerk.

Stage 3: This is progressively deeper sleep. You become more difficult to arouse and are not initially functional if aroused at this stage.

Stage 4: This phase is characterized by a very deep sleep. You are very difficult to arouse at this point. You will stay in this phase until you transition into REM sleep or period of rapid eye motion.

REM Sleep

Following the first four stages of sleep, the body progresses into REM sleep where the brain activity resembles being awake. This is where your dreaming begins. The body is now completely immobile and in a state of paralysis. This immobility is important since the body cannot react to what is going on in the mind through the dreaming experience. Can you imagine having a nightmare where you experience yourself running? Without the paralysis associated with this level of sleep, you may actually run----into a wall. There are however people that suffer with problems such as sleepwalking. Sleepwalking can be a very dangerous sleep disorder that can lead to physical injury. Imagine if your body was allowed to act out your dreams?

Body functions such as blood pressure, pulse rate, temperature, and respiratory rates are also going to change during this stage of sleep. It is believed that the REM stage of sleep allows for the mind to process the experiences of the day and to mentally work out conflicts and ideas. All of these cycles are necessary for the body to feel rested.

Sleep Deprivation

Sleep deprivation is the lack of sleep, which leads to a decrease in body and mental function. There is a marked decrease in the ability of the body to perform both simple and complex tasks of the physical and mental variety. The body becomes less efficient and accurate.

There is also a decrease in the ability to concentrate when sleep deprived. Remember the days when you used to cram for tests, or maybe you still do? You actually reduce your chance to do well on exams if you cram to the point of exhaustion. Mental acuity drops so you will not only forget the new material you crammed but will also be less accurate and less effective in the recall of the material you thought you knew.

Losing sleep also increases the degree of physical and mental irritability, which can lead to mood swings. Road rage and violent acts can be triggered by this irritability. Irritability can also override rational thought.

Inefficient sleep also decreases the effectiveness of the immune system and limits the body's ability to ward off infections and diseases. We have talked about the importance of the immune system in previous chapters. Consistently getting enough sleep is one way to help boost the immune system to remain strong and responsive.

In the most severe of situations, persistent sleep deprivation can lead to hallucinations and, although rare, has been linked to death. Although most of us will never experience the extreme, sleep deprivation can have a profound effect on our life.

Sleep Debt

Can you catch up on sleep? This has been a debate in the literature for a long time, but it seems that the experts now believe the answer is yes. Sleep debt is very much like financial debt; at some time, you need to pay it back. The less sleep you get, and the more active you are, the more you accumulate what is called sleep debt. The need for sleep and the accumulation of your sleep debt increases as the day progresses. For instance, you wake up in morning and feel pretty rested. By evening, you notice that you are beginning to feel a little tired. The longer you go without adequate sleep, the greater your sleep debt becomes. The greatest incident of sleep debt has been identified in new parents, students, and people that work non-traditional shifts.

Those of you who have had children can easily relate to this especially in the first few weeks when babies are up throughout the night. I remember times with my kids that I would do just about anything for a couple hours of sleep. Students have some similar, although self-inflicted, experiences with late night studying sessions and extensive partying.

Shift work is counter to the reality of our Circadian rhythms although there is need for round the clock work in many organizations. Much research has been targeted to this population of employees, most of it suggests that adaptation to these hours is very difficult and in some cases adaptation to this type of schedule is impossible for most people. It is important for these individuals to do their best to keep a consistent sleep schedule and to outfit the room that they rest in with darkening blinds. It is also important to sound proof the room as much as possible by keeping the door closed and by turning off the ringers on phones. As a new nurse, I worked the critical care unit on the midnight shift and found it impossible for me to adjust to this schedule. I found myself chronically fatigued and ill, and I did not begin to feel better until I switched to a day shift schedule. I remember taking my lunch breaks and sleeping in the lounge in order to make it through my shift.

Recently, the notion of sleep debt has received much attention in hospitals and healthcare organizations in response to mistakes made in the clinical setting that can lead to injury or death of patients. Residents and medical students now have limitations on how many hours they can work in one day in order to prevent medical errors due to sleep deprivation and fatigue. Risk associated to sleep debt is the reason that there are strict regulations that do not allow pilots or flight attendants to fly longer than a certain amount of hours. Similar regulations exist in the trucking industry preventing drivers from becoming overtired and unreliable on the road.

The good news is that it is easy to repay your sleep debt. Simply sleep longer to catch up. Most people adjust their sleep patterns to pay back their sleep debt on their own. If you are really tired, you will go to bed early or sleep later if you can. You can also try to take a small nap in mid-afternoon if possible in cases of extreme fatigue. Many people feel that they have to catch up by sleeping longer on the weekend.

While I was doing research for this chapter, I realized how sleep deprived I have been because of my demanding schedule. I began to make a conscious effort to allow myself to wake up on the weekends without an alarm whenever possible. I find that when I can do this I feel more rested throughout the week. I notice that there are days I sleep ten hours and then there are times I sleep twelve hours. If I have worked out heavily through the week, I find that I need more sleep. If I allow my body to self-regulate sleep patterns, it will do that very effectively. Yours will also.

How Much Is Enough?

How much sleep do you need depends on several variables, the first of which is your own personal, internal rhythms. Some people can function very well with five hours of sleep whereby others need nine to ten hours of sleep. During growth periods, children and teens will sleep longer due to the excretion of growth hormones and rest needed for physical growth. Your personal activity level will also determine how much sleep you need. For those of you that exercise quite a bit, excessive exercise or high levels of physical activity will increase your need for sleep and increase the time needed for physical recovery for muscles, joints, and bones. Fatigue caused by emotional stress can also add to the need for sleep.

It has also been said that we will need to sleep less as we get older. This is generally not true. Decreased sleep is usually a result of decreased activity. Active older adults need recovery time also. The length and rhythms of our sleep cycles may change with age, although the overall sleep requirements do not.

How do you find how much sleep you need? There are a couple of techniques for you to find your optimal sleep needs. You may want to try both of these techniques when you have time to do so such as a weekend or days that you don't have a demanding schedule. I recommend that you use them both.

The first technique is to sleep long enough to wake up on your own without an alarm. If you have a rare, nice weekend coming up where you don't have to get out of bed at any particular time, sleep until you wake without the alarm. Remember approximately when you went to bed and then when you woke up, and simply count the hours. Do this a few times to identify a rhythm.

The next technique is to identify whether you feel rested as an indicator of enough sleep. On the days that you wake and feel rested, count the hours of sleep that you have received and compare them to your other experience of waking without the alarm. If you have slept eight hours and you still feel tired and not ready for the day, you probably require more than your usual hours of sleep a night.

There are times in your life when you may not be able to get enough rest. An example is menopause. For all peri-menopausal and menopausal women, sleep can become illusive and a challenge. All bets are off with your sleeping patterns. Women during this phase of life report an increase in sleep deprivation. This may be a result of several hormonal changes that alter sleep patterns and result in waking during the middle of the night. Waking can also result from discomfort due to hot flashes. Your gynecologist is your best resource to help your sleep problems through the menopause years. This is just something that we have to deal with as women.

Sleep Disorders

The science of sleep is beginning to unlock many of the mysteries of what happens to us when we sleep and some of the reasons for sleep problem. More and more physicians in the area of sleep are identifying physical problems that can contribute to sleep deprivation. Treatments for these conditions are available and improving at a steady rate. If you believe you have a sleep disorder or continue to have signs of sleep deprivation, see your physician to evaluate whether you need to see a specialist for follow up testing. Sometimes, sleep problems can be resolved very simply with simple lifestyle changes such as changes in diet or the purchase of a new bed. Stress management or personal life changes can also help. There are, however, serious medical conditions such as sleep apnea that can be dangerous to your health, which can be corrected with the appropriate treatment. My advice is always when in doubt, check it out and seek the advice of a professional.

Directions: Evaluate Your Sleep Quality

Your exercise for this chapter is quick and easy. Simply read through the checklist and answer Yes or No to the questions listed. Review your answers, and if you have answered Yes to any of them, you may need to explore ways to improve your sleep rhythms. It is important for you to go back to your first exercise on rhythms and count the number of hours you are sleeping every night. See if you are allowing for catch up sleep at any time. Ponder what you think you can do to incorporate more sleep into your life.

CHAPTER 9 EXERCISE: SLEEP EVALUATION TOOL

	Sleep Elevation	Yes	No
1	Do you regularly sleep less than six hours a night?		
2	Do you frequently feel tired through the day?		
3	Do you have regular periods of dozing through the day?		
4	Do you frequently have trouble falling asleep at night?		
5	Do you frequently have trouble staying asleep at night?		
6	Do you frequently feel irritated because you are tired?		
7	Do you frequently have trouble concentrating because you are tired?		
8	Do you frequently feel less productive at work because you are tired?		
9	Do you feel comfortable in your bed?		

If you have answered Yes to any of these questions, and these conditions persist, you may need to follow up with your physician to have the status of your sleep evaluated.

Next Steps

Take some time to reflect on this chapter and make some positive changes in your sleep rhythms with your new knowledge. Although it seems simple, this can be challenging. We are now moving into the third topic of our Trifecta of health, which is nutrition.

TAP DANCE INSTRUCTION: THE WALTZ CLOG

This next step is called the waltz clog and is perfect to include after a discussion of sleep since it is performed very slowly and has a very rhythmic, soothing rhythm. To begin, you step on one foot and then shuffle your other foot out and back. Lastly, do a ball change (weight on your left toe, then step back on the right foot) with the opposite foot, alternate from side-by-side in a slow, soothing rhythm.

CHAPTER 10:
NUTRITIONAL RHYTHMS; IT'S EASIER THAN YOU THINK

OBJECTIVES: CHAPTER 10

1. Learn about good nutrition

2. Understand how good nutrition relates to good health

3. Learn tips to improve your nutrition the easy way

4. Identify your personal eating rhythms

What is Good Nutrition?

Good nutrition is simply eating a variety of good foods that provide the body with appropriate nutrients to grow and repair. There are three important factors to remember when thinking about nutrition. These are variety, balance, and moderation. Incorporating these factors into our dietary choices will help to ensure that we are eating the appropriate mix of nutrients for overall health and energy.

Variety

Variety simply means to mix up your food choices among various food groups. We oftentimes find that we settle into eating rhythms that are easy and enjoyable for us. The problem is that we can become so set in these rhythms that we will not be eating a complete diet. There is no one perfect food that provides all of the nutrients that we need no matter how complete we have heard the food is. It is very important for us to get the variety, to be able to meet the demands and needs of our body.

Balance

The second important component in a complete diet is balance. Balance refers to the right amounts of food coupled with the variety we spoke of earlier. These foods can be found on any food pyramid along with the recommended portions. A balanced diet will help us eat not only the right foods but also the right mix of calories as well as the complete requirements for total nutrients.

Moderation

There are no "bad" foods if eaten in moderation. Even the ingestion of alcohol is alright in moderation. High fat foods such as chips, candies, and French fries can be easily managed in a diet as long as we follow the principle of moderation. For instance, the recommended serving for potato chips is eleven. How many times have you eaten only eleven chips? In my own experience I could say never!

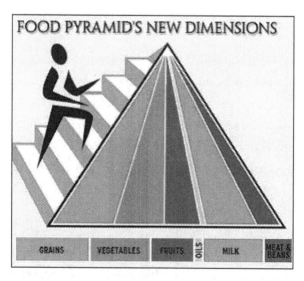

U.S. Department of Agriculture

The New Food Pyramid

The food pyramid is a wonderful guide to help you select a very well balanced eating plan that has the appropriate amount of calories and nutrients for you. There are many food pyramids available for review all of which provide you similar information. The U.S. Department of Agriculture recently released the New Food Pyramid, which is very different from the old. The goal of the new pyramid is to simplify the concept and include the importance of exercise in order to create a new system to help Americans lead healthier lives. Perhaps the old food pyramid was too much of a "science project" that was difficult to understand and practice. The new one is very simple. There also is an interactive web site to help you individualize your own pyramid. Here is how the pyramid works.

Exercise

Review of the pyramid shows an individual walking up a set of stairs to replicate the need for exercise in our lives. Of course, you all know that now that you reviewed the chapter on exercise. It is a sad truth, however, that great numbers of Americans do not exercise, nor do they see the connection between exercise and health.

Band 1: Whole Grains

This band is orange on the pyramid and represents whole grains. The key here is the word whole. It is recommended that we limit our complex carbohydrates, and eat about three ounces a day of whole grain products such as breads, rice, or pasta. Stay away from bleached and white products such as white bread, rice and pasta.

Band 2: Vegetables

This band is green on the pyramid and represents vegetables. Vegetables add very few calories in the diet yet are full of fiber and vitamins. The recommendation is to eat more dark green and orange vegetables. It is also recommended to increase your intake of legumes (bean and peas), which also adds fiber and protein.

Band 3: Fruits

This band is red on the pyramid and represents the fruit family. As with vegetables, fruits add very little in the way of calories to the diet. It is recommended to eat a variety of fruits, preferably fresh, and to limit the intake of fruit juice. Juice is concentrated and therefore has more calories than the fruit and may lack the fiber.

Band 4: Oils

The smallest band on the pyramid represents the oils and fats category. It is critically important for a low fat diet to limit the intake of fats and oils. Plant oils such as olive, canola, soy, sunflower, and peanut are the best. We will discuss more about fats later.

Band 5: Milk and Dairy

This band is blue and represents calcium rich foods such as dairy products. It is recommended to ingest dairy products that are low fat or fat free. This also includes cheese, yogurts and other products made from milk. If you are lactose intolerant, there are lactose-free products or other calcium supplements available.

Band 6: Meat and Beans

This band is purple and represents meat and beans, both of which provide protein in the diet. It is recommended to severely limit red meat and eat more chicken and fish. Baking, broiling, or grilling your meat further decreases the fat ingested. Beans, peas, nuts, and seeds are also considered important for the increase of protein in the diet.

Portion Size

Many of the problems with high calorie intake are not necessarily due to what we are eating but rather the portion size that we are eating. For instance, a serving of bread is one slice. The serving size for most high fat snacks is one ounce. The serving size for cheese is usually a slice or one ounce. Serving sizes can be found on food labels of all the products you buy. You also need to be aware of the number of servings per food container. You could say that a serving of canned soup is only one hundred calories, but the can contains 2.5 servings, which would be 250 calories. Another example is pasta, which is good for us to eat, but how often do we have only one cup of pasta? One cup of pasta is usually the recommended serving size. Pay attention to serving size with everything you eat. One way to begin reducing your calorie intake is to cut back your serving size just a bit on everything that you are eating. This can add up to hundreds of saved calories a day. Remember that one pound of weight is 3500 calories. In other words, to loose one pound of fat I need to reduce my caloric intake by 3500 calories or burn 3500 calories with physical activity. Reducing calorie intake by even 200 calories a day and adding physical activity three times a week could burn and eliminate 2000 calories a week! You could easily lose one pound every two weeks without even feeling the pain!!

Components of a Healthy Diet

A healthy diet is all about proper nutrients and several components contribute to this total approach to healthy eating. Understanding these components will help you make good choices and manage your calorie intake. We will review all of them in detail.

Carbohydrates

The largest group of food in our diet is carbohydrates. It is recommended to include six to eleven servings in your daily diet. Carbohydrates are a very important part of a healthy diet, even though they sometimes get a bad rap from fad diet supporters. In fact, carbohydrates, in of themselves, have only four calories per gram ingested. Carbohydrates are basically sugar molecules, which provide necessary energy for the body, and helps the body achieve optimum physical activity and endurance. In order for the body to use this energy, carbohydrates are broken down in the digestive system into single sugar molecules, which are then absorbed in the bloodstream to be stored or utilized. Without adequate energy your body will feel fatigued. Fruits, vegetables, breads, rice and pastas are in the carbohydrate group.

Glycemic Index

The glycemic index is becoming more recognizable for its importance in the selection of the carbohydrates we eat. The glycemic index refers to the speed that the body breaks down the carbohydrate to a simple sugar and then processes it in the body. Refined carbohydrates like white bread, white rice, bleached flower and high sugar snacks have a very high glycemic index. These carbohydrates break down very quickly in the digestive track and as a result increase the blood sugar, insulin secretion, and the storage of fat. Conversely, high fiber breads, fruits, and vegetables break down more slowly, reducing your blood sugar, insulin requirements and fat storage.

Carbohydrate Pitfalls

There are two important pitfalls in response to carbohydrate selection apart from the glycemic index, which include portion size and what we do to the carbohydrates to make them flavorful.

For instance, a baked potato is very low in fat and calories. The problem is, most of us never eat a plain baked potato? We usually dress up the potato with butter, sour cream, cheese or other toppings to make them exciting to eat, all of which adds unnecessary calories.

The second pitfall is the fact that it is common to eat more food volume than what is necessary. As mentioned before, a serving of pasta is one cup whereby a serving of potato chips is one ounce and a serving of crackers might be four. I don't remember the last time I ate only one ounce of potato chips. In fact, put the bag in front of me and chances are it will be gone soon—I am a salt lover and chips are my downfall. Controlling portions and watching what we add to our carbohydrates is the key to reducing our calories.

Protein

Protein is also a very important component of a healthy diet. Like carbohydrates, protein foods provide only four calories per gram of protein eaten. Proteins are made up of amino acids, which are important for growth, development, sustaining muscle tissue and increasing immunity. Sources of protein include fish, meats, dairy, eggs, cheese, nuts, peanut butter, and tofu products. Complete proteins can also be created through the combination of some legumes especially important in vegetarian diets.

There are requirements for the amount of protein we need in our diet, and it is not as much as you think. Experts recommend the intake of one gram of protein per kilogram of body weight, or nine grams for every twenty pounds on a daily basis is all that is needed to be healthy. For a 150-pound individual, that would be 150 divided by 20 and multiplied by 9, or 67.5 grams of protein. There are about 28.34 grams of protein per ounce of meat product. A six-ounce chicken breast (without the skin) would be 170 grams of protein, so it is relatively easy to get your recommended daily allowance of protein. Once again, to identify the amount of protein you are eating, read your food labels. For meat, poultry, and fish products, you can get this information from a nutrition handbook (there are several great ones available at book stores) or use the Internet.

Protein metabolizes differently in the body than carbohydrates. First of all, protein is generally slower to empty from the stomach than carbohydrates, which makes you feel full longer. Think back to a big steak dinner you had, and compare it to when you had a salad or vegetable combination for dinner or even pasta dishes made without meat. You probably felt hungry sooner in the absence of protein from a meal due to the speed of digestion. There is also not a rapid increase in blood sugar, so there is not the large insulin bolus in the body. Lastly, the body uses more energy from metabolized proteins than fats or carbohydrates because of the complex absorption process.

Protein Pitfalls

We also have some pitfalls with protein. First of all, some proteins can be loaded with fat. Beef for instance, depending on the cut, can be very fatty. Chicken is generally low in fat if your remove the skin. It is recommended to remove all sources of visible fat and to limit your intake of fatty, red meats to twice a week. Red meat can be substituted in the diet by pork, chicken, fish, or tofu.

Portion size is also important. The size of a steak should not be any larger than the palm of your hand or four ounces. The size of steaks in better restaurants begin with 6ounces and sometimes are as large as 12 ounces. Portion size for chicken is also four ounces, which is a very small chicken breast.

What we add to our proteins can also increase the number of calories. Ketchup is mostly sugar and can add calories to those burgers. Creamy sauces on meats can also add calories. The way we prepare protein can reduce fat and decrease calories. For example, grilled meats allow for the drainage of fat off the meat. I find that I can reduce fat in ground beef dishes by browning the hamburger and then rinsing all of the visible fat with water before adding seasonings and preparing the meal. Deep-frying should always be eliminated no matter what you are preparing.

Fats

Not all fats are bad, and fats are an important part of healthy diet. They are necessary for several body functions such as the formation of cell membranes, which protect the integrity of the cell, and important for the manufacturing of hormones, which are responsible for growth and regulatory functions. There are two general problems with fat. First of all, we eat too many foods that are high in fat. We also eat too many bad fats versus good fats.

Only twenty-five percent of our daily calories should come from fat, yet the American diet usually has up to seventy-five percent of calories from fat. If I eat 2,000 calories of food in a day, only 500 calories should be from fat. A serving of potato chips may be only 150 calories, but when you look at the serving size, ninety percent of those calories are coming from fat. You have already used 135 calories of the 500 calories available for fat so, fats, unlike proteins and carbohydrates, are a little bit more expensive to eat. There are nine calories per gram of fat ingested, which is more than double what you take in with carbohydrates and protein.

Good Fat Vs. Bad Fat

Not all fats are created equal in respect to the effects of fat on the body. Research has linked bad fats, or trans-fats and saturated fats, to increased risk of disease. Good fats, also known as mono-saturated and polyunsaturated fats, lower the risk of disease. It is important, whenever possible, to replace the bad fats in your diet with the good fats. Some of the good fats are foods like olive oil, canola, peanut, corn, soy, safflower, cottonseed oils, nuts, avocados, and fish. Fats that you should limit in your diet are foods like whole milk, butter, cheese, meat, chocolate, ice cream (all the good stuff, right?), coconut products, margarine, fast food, fried snack foods, vegetable shortening and baked goods such as cookies and cakes. These fats are responsible for the increase in the body's cholesterol level, which can clog the arteries and lead to disease. Heredity may also play a part in high cholesterol levels, which can be compounded by the addition of fatty foods in the diet.

Cholesterol

Cholesterol is a wax-like substance that is found in the bloodstream and necessary for the strength of the cell membranes and hormone production. It is very important for vital bodily functions; however the body has a process to manufacture cholesterol in the liver, so there really is no medical reason to ingest more. Foods high in cholesterol can result in an excess of this waxy substance building up in the arteries. This waxy build up slows down circulation, increases the resistance in the blood vessels and can lead to blood clot formation. Diseases associated with high cholesterol include hypertension, cardiac disease, strokes, heart attacks, diabetes, cancer, and kidney disease.

HDL/LDL

The body does however have a mechanism to remove excess cholesterol from the system. You have probably heard the terms HDL and LDL in relation to diet and health. These are carriers of cholesterol in the body, and they work in opposition and perform different processes. HDL or high-density lipoprotein is the cleanup crew, which moves cholesterol from the bloodstream to the liver for appropriate storage. The higher the HDL, the cleaner the arteries and cardiovascular system will be. We can increase HDL in our system by doing things such as exercising and eating a healthy diet.

LDL, or low-density lipoprotein, is the carrier of cholesterol that moves it from the liver to the rest of the body. A high LDL level coupled with a low HDL level can lead to clogged arteries and or all of the diseases mentioned above. It is like cleaning your kid's room. You put things away and when you return they throw things all around again. What is important for health is to have a good ratio of HDL to LDL to keep a healthy balance and prevent fatty deposits in the body.

The best approach is to decrease your fat intake as much as possible. You can do this by selecting low-fat foods, decreasing the use of butters, margarines, and condiments such as mayonnaise, as well as decreasing your intake of fried and fast food. It is also helpful to be aware of hidden fats such as marbling in meat products, chicken skin and all of the fat in processed and snack foods.

Fiber

Fiber has been getting a lot of good press lately for its benefits to a healthy diet. Fiber has two primary functions in the body. First of all, it absorbs fat in the gastrointestinal system and provides a cleansing process to help move food through the bowel. It has been documented that that eating fiber decreases your risk of cardiac disease, diabetes and some diseases of the bowel such as diverticulosis (an out pouching of the intestines). For years, it was also believed that fiber could decrease the incidence of colon cancer; however there are some studies that suggest that this may not be true. Further study is necessary to establish a conclusion on that theory.

Types of fiber

There are two types of fiber in food: soluble and insoluble. Whether the fiber is soluble or insoluble refers to how fast the fiber dissolves in water. Soluble fibers are those foods that dissolve more quickly in water and include things like oatmeal, fruit, lentils, beans and peas, nuts, and oat bran. The insoluble fibers do not dissolve in water and include foods such as whole grains, wheat, vegetables, barley, brown rice, and tomatoes. It is necessary to include both types of fiber in the diet.

How Much Fiber Do We Need?

It is recommended that adults consume twenty-five to thirty-five grams of fiber per day. Unfortunately, the average diet contains only about fifteen percent of fiber. Adding fiber to the diet can be as simple as converting white breads to whole wheat, exchanging brown rice for white rice, and attempting to eliminate as much processed foods as possible. There are also many very palatable fiber substitutes on the marked from wafers to liquids to choose from. It is very important to include more fiber in our diets.

Water

You may not even think of water as a nutrient, but it is one of the most critical yet most ignored components of a healthy lifestyle. Many people live their lives in a state of dehydration despite the fact that water is so important for the maintenance of healthy life rhythms. Next to air, water is the second most necessary element of life. The human body can survive for several weeks without food but only a couple of days without water.

Function of Water in the Body

Our bodies are about sixty to seventy percent water, depending on body size and the amount of muscle mass. Water contributes to all physiological functions in the body. Have you ever looked at a pond that is drying up and cracking? What about a lawn that has not had enough water or flowers that dry up and die? The same thing happens to the body when we are not drinking enough water. Suddenly I am feeling thirsty!!

Water is responsible for several activities in the body including:

- Maintenance of adequate blood volume and circulation

- Temperature regulation

- Elasticity of the skin

- Oxygen exchange in the lungs

- The whole activity of breathing

- Healthy immune system

- Adequate brain function

- Lubrication of joints

- Healthy, firm muscles and bones

- Kidney function

- Digestion.

- Removal of excess body fat and many more

So, what happens if we don't drink enough water? Without enough water, our bodies begin to dry up and vital functions shut down. Blood pressure, heart rate, and respiratory rate go up, muscles and joints become sore and our urine output drops due to decreased activity of the kidney. The body actually becomes increasingly toxic due to the buildup all the byproducts that are not being removed because there is no water to pass them out of the system. Notice the color of your urine on days that you have not been drinking water and notice how dark it becomes. Now look at the color of your urine when you are drinking enough water and it should be a light, clear yellow.

The Gastrointestinal system slows down, our mucus membranes dry up, the skin becomes dry, body temperature increases and we lose our mental clarity. These changes in the body begin when there is a decrease of ten percent of body fluids. This is also the time when you become thirsty. It is important to remember that when you are thirsty you are already seriously behind in your fluids. To keep ahead of your fluid needs, you need to drink water regularly whether you are thirsty or not and replace fluids continuously when you work outdoors or exercise. The recommendation for fluid replacement with activity is one eight-ounce glass of water before you begin activity and three to four ounces of fluid every twenty minutes throughout the activity. Of course, the amount of water you need increases in very hot climates.

How Much Water Should I drink?

You need to drink a minimum of eight to ten, eight ounce glasses of water per day. Water intake should be greater if you are physically active (as described above), in excessive heat conditions or if you are experiencing illness or gastrointestinal problems like diarrhea. Always replace fluids immediately when you begin to feel thirsty.

What Should I Drink?

It is always better to drink water to replace fluids. Many of the other drinks that are available, such as juice and sport drinks, are made with water so they will give you some degree of rehydration. The problem with this is that fluids like juice and soda also provide sugars, which contribute to dehydration because of the increase of sugar in the blood. Coffees and teas also provide water, but they also provide caffeine, which is a diuretic that increases urine output and further dehydrates the body. You may think that you are getting your fluids with these choices but you are actually negating the benefit by loosing more fluids. Before choosing a drink for fluid replacement, check the label of the drink to make sure that the fluid is ninety percent water or greater.

Weight Loss & Water

Hydration is a very important component of our weight loss program. We will not lose fat from the body unless there is enough water. There are two important reasons to drink water if you are trying to lose weight. First of all, you lose weight because your body metabolizes fats for energy when you reduce your calories and increase your exercise. In order to metabolize the fat, the body needs two components: water and oxygen. If you are dehydrated, the body will choose to retain the fat and metabolize protein instead.

The second reason that water is so important to weight loss is what happens in the brain with our hunger and thirst alert centers. They are one in the same. If you feel thirsty you may be hungry, and if you are hungry you may be thirsty. This is easy to figure out. If you feel hungry before you eat anything, try to drink a glass of water first. If this does not eliminate your hunger, then you probably need to eat. Following these two tips will help you with your fat reduction goal.

Vitamins

The topic of vitamins is extensive and very complex so we will only briefly discuss them here. There is so much research and so many varied opinions that this topic can also be very confusing. It can also be dangerous to ingest high doses of vitamins. What is important to know is that vitamins are elements necessary for your body rhythms, which the body cannot manufacture themselves and therefore need to be ingested either in your foods or by supplementation. They provide a catalyst for many processes that take place in the body. It is best and more natural to get vitamins from food. It is possible for you to receive all the vitamins you need from your food, if you are eating a well-balanced diet, especially since you need such small amounts. Unfortunately, most people don't eat a diet rich in all the vitamins. Experts now believe that it is beneficial to supplement your diet with a multivitamin. Stay away from the media hype, infomercials, and ads that promise great results with high vitamin dosages, and ask your doctor what is the best vitamin choice for you. Taking high concentrations of vitamins can lead to the development of certain toxicities that might actually do more harm than good to your body and, in extreme cases, can be fatal. This can be more dangerous with the ingestion of the fat-soluble vitamins, A, D, E and K but toxicity can be associated with overdoses of the water-soluble vitamins C and B complex. Research and a quick discussion with your physician will keep you on the right track with vitamins.

Minerals

Like vitamins, minerals function as a catalyst for body processes, and also provide the body with building blocks that promote growth and maintain strength. Minerals also need to be ingested and are not manufactured in the body. The mineral that seems to get the most attention is calcium. Calcium is necessary for strong bones and teeth, and is also important for other body functions such as electrical activity of the heart, blood clotting and the activity of the nervous system. Calcium is so vital to life that if we don't get enough calcium through our diet, the body begins to pull calcium from our bones, which is a rich supply of ready calcium. Over time, this can result in severe weakening of the bone known as osteoporosis, a serious problem especially for older women who are losing calcium from the bones due to hormonal changes. It is important to note that osteoporosis is not only a disease of older women but can also be a problem for older men and individuals with eating disorders or digestive absorption diseases.

It has long been the recommendation to replace calcium by drinking milk and eating dairy products. Milk and dairy products are the richest source of Calcium, but they also can bring unnecessary fat into the diet. Choose the low-fat options such as skimmed milk, low fat yogurt, and cheese. Calcium can also be replaced with supplements. Your doctor is the best source of information for the type and the dosage of Calcium.

Potassium is another mineral vital to body function, especially in muscle efficiency and electrical activity of the heart. If you have a form of cardiac disease, Potassium is critical, especially in balance with drugs that you are taking. Your doctor should be the one to prescribe Potassium supplements since toxicity of this mineral can be fatal.

Alcohol

Although not a nutrient, it is very important to include alcohol in a discussion of nutrition to try to answer some of the questions about the benefits or dangers. Research suggest that in moderate amounts, there may be some health advantages to moderate drinking which include the increase in HDL, stress reduction, improved cardiac and circulatory system health as well as protection against type-II diabetes.

The key to whether alcohol is beneficial to our bodies is the amount that we drink. In large amounts, alcohol is a poison that can become toxic to the heart, stomach, GI system, liver, brain and nervous system, and it has been linked to some cancers. There is also a risk of dependency that can lead to alcoholism. Drunk driving is the number one cause of fatal automobile accidents. Alcohol as a drug cannot be taken lightly.

How Much is Safe?

There are recommendations for how much alcohol might be safe. The U.S. department of agriculture has identified these following guidelines. Men should not ingest more than one to two drinks a day. One drink a day for women is expected to be safe.

The definition of a drink is also important to know. A drink according to the above guidelines is defined as a twelve-ounce beer, five ounces of wine, or one and a half ounces of hard liquor. This should equate to no more than twelve to fourteen grams of alcohol in total. The greater message is to drink responsibly and pay attention to the amount of alcohol you ingest to keep it at a safe level. Also, never drink and drive. Alcohol and driving can be your one fatal mistake that can have far-reaching effects on your life and the lives of others.

Tips for Healthy Diet

Eating a healthy diet does not have to be that challenging if you are aware of some tips to help you. Here are several recommendations to help you make healthy changes in your nutritional rhythms and keep you on track to your goals.

Moderate Alcohol Intake

As mentioned before, there are advantages to small amounts of alcohol in the diet. The reverse is true when alcohol consumption increases. Apart from the toxicity possible with higher alcohol ingestion, these drinks are also loaded with wasted calories and can lead to weight gain.

There is No Magic Potion for Weight Loss

Please remember that there is no magic potion for losing weight. The only successful approach is eating well, exercising, drinking water, and getting your rest. Ads about magic pills and potions for weight loss are designed to do **nothing** but make the manufactures of these products rich! They hook you to buy their products by telling you what they want you to hear that would entice you to purchase the products. It works! Diet aids are an incredibly lucrative industry, which does not contribute to quality health. Without proper regulation you don't even know if what you are taking is safe. The individuals you may see on the commercials are all actors, so it is their job to convince you of the benefits of the product. I worked for seven years in television marketing and sales, so I am familiar with these strategies. There has been no evidence to suggest that there is any magic pill out there for you to lose weight. You just have to keep your nose to the grindstone and make moderate changes in your diet and lifestyle over time.

Eliminate Fat From Your Diet

Eliminate fried foods and fat wherever you can. Substitute fried foods with grilled or baked. Fat brings calories. Also limit your use of high-fat condiments such as mayonnaise. Lastly cut off or remove all visible fat such as skin on chicken and fat on meat products. All of these approaches will decrease your fat intake and decrease your calories.

Healthy Snacking

Eat whole fruits and vegetables for snacks and keep your house stocked with good choices. If you don't have good choices handy in the house, you will gravitate to foods that are easy to eat and can be high in fat. It is also helpful to carry a low calorie, low fat snack with you such as a granola bar or piece of fruit. This will help to curb your appetite and cut down on binge eating.

Low Calorie Fluids

You can limit your calorie intake by drinking low calorie fluids. I am not recommending that you drink a lot of diet sodas. Diet sodas have other problems with the artificial sweeteners and excessive sodium. Increase your water intake as the number one choice of fluid to drink, and read your labels before you buy.

Low Fat Dairy Products

Use low-fat dairy products. Whole milks and cheese have many extra calories because of the fat. Convert to skimmed and low fat alternatives.

Read Your Labels

Always read your labels so you know what you are buying and what you are eating. Labels can say thirty percent fat free but may still have a high calorie count.

Portion Control

One of the biggest problems we have with our diet rhythms is portion control. Everything now-a-days is super-sized. Right? For thirty-nine cents, you can super size your whole meal. The problem is that even before super-sizing that portion is probably twice what you should be eating and sometimes even three times the calories. Be aware of portions of snack food, and try to keep to the recommendation.

Increase Your Complex Carbohydrates

Replace your refined products with whole grains such as wheat bread instead of white, wheat pasta instead of white, whole grain crackers instead of regular, and eat whole grain cereals. These foods have a lower glycemic index and will provide more fiber.

Keep a Diet Diary

A very successful way to identify your dietary rhythms and stay accountable to your goals for a healthy diet is to write down what you eat and review it on a daily basis. There is something magical about having to write down the fact that you ate two or three candy bars when you know you shouldn't have. This will also give you a chance to calculate your calories and balance your meals.

Limit Refined Sugars

Get those candies, cookies and sodas out of your life. They have absolutely no nutritional value and are all wasted calories.

Moderation/Gradual Changes

Making lasting positive changes in your diet and nutrition is all about moderation and gradual change. We have to slowly change those rhythms and bad habits that have evolved over time. Here is an example of a change I made with my family. With my first child, our family became used to drinking whole milk. When my son was older and didn't need the advantages of whole milk any longer, I wanted to begin to eliminate some fat sources in all of our diets. We tried skimmed milk, and my son and husband hated it and refused to drink it. They had every excuse for why not to drink it. It tasted bad, it looked like water, it was clear, it was bland, and on and on. I tried buying only skimmed milk to force the issue, but this would routinely sour over time. I thought that I would try something a little different. I bought a gallon of whole milk, emptied a quarter of it and filled it with skimmed milk. We drank this mix for a couple of weeks and no one seemed to notice. I then emptied a half a gallon and mixed it with a half a gallon of the skimmed. Once again, we drank it for a couple of weeks and no one seemed to notice this either. I reduced the whole milk to one quarter whole and three quarters skimmed and eventually converted to all skimmed.

After we had been drinking skimmed for a while I put the skimmed milk on the table and heard the revolt as before. I told them that we had been drinking skimmed milk for a while now and that they didn't even notice. When they tasted the skimmed milk, they realized that this was what they were drinking and skimmed milk became the preferred choice. I also used the same strategy with the conversion from regular sodas to diet.

The point that I am trying to make is that wholesale, cold turkey changes in our lives can be overwhelming and lead to perceptions of failure. Making changes little by little is not only manageable but also a way to have changes become accepted parts of our lives.

Status of Nutrition in the U.S.

As a society, we are not doing very well in the area of nutrition and dietary rhythms. The latest statistics from the National Center for Health Statistics show that thirty percent of all people in the U.S. are obese. Less than twenty-five percent of all people eat a healthy diet and fifty percent of the U.S. population does not exercise. Our kids are the fattest kids in the world with only one third of all of our children engaging in physical activity. This is a sad state of affairs for us and points us down the path of a society that will eventually suffer chronic diseases at epidemic proportions. Diabetes is already reaching epidemic proportions. Our already burdened healthcare system cannot take this pressure. In my experience, lifestyle diseases are agonizing and a horrible way to die. Believe me, I have watched many people suffer unnecessarily. Only we can change that destiny by focusing on our personal health and the health of those around us. It takes us a long time to get out of shape and gain weight, so it will take time to get back in shape but it can be done! Be good to yourself, and give yourself time to get back to a healthy state. Make these changes in moderation over time and they will eventually become part of your healthy rhythms.

Directions: Diet Diary

The exercise for this chapter is called a diet diary. I designed it to help you identify your particular diet rhythms and make you aware of where changes can be made. Keep this diet diary for one week to get a good sampling of seven days of eating.

For the course of the week, whatever you put in your mouth should be logged on the diary. For instance, you eat a bowl of oatmeal for breakfast. Log in the date, time, what was eaten and how much. In this case, it could be six am oatmeal, one bowl for breakfast. There is also a section for comments if you want to jot down something unusual about the entry. Perhaps you had a candy bar and you want to comment that you felt stressed or depressed, and that is what prompted you to make that choice. Also, if you feel bad about eating something log that as well. Try to get as much insight into your personal eating rhythms as you can.

Be honest with yourself and write down every single thing you eat. Even if you are baking brownies for the kids and you lick the bowl or the spatula a couple times, write it down. These incidental calories add up.

After the two weeks, go back and review your rhythms. Look at the times you usually eat, any particular pattern in what you eat (such as fast food stops) and any particular activity that seems to align with eating. This could be something like watching TV.

Try to identify anything that you think can and should change. If you eat when you watch TV, then maybe you want to do something while you watch TV to prevent you from eating, or maybe you want to substitute TV for another activity to prevent you from eating.

You may find that you have a pattern or a tendency to snack on unhealthy things when you get home from work. You may want to keep an apple in your car to curb your appetite and prevent binge eating when you get home.

Look at the type of foods that you're eating and if you're frequenting fast food restaurants. Or, if you're eating other unhealthy foods, think about how to change those activities.

Fast food restaurants have been adding some low-fat choices. If you need to eat at a fast food restaurant substitute high fat burgers for grilled chicken sandwiches and eliminate the fries. Fast food restaurants now provide nutritional information.

(see charts on pages 149-151)

CHAPTER 10 EXERCISE: ANALYZE YOUR DIET

Diet Diary

Date	Time	Food Eaten	Estimated Portion	Estimated Calories	Activity

CHAPTER 10 EXERCISE: ANALYZE YOUR DIET

Diet Diary

Date	Time	Food Eaten	Estimated Portion	Estimated Calories	Activity

CHAPTER 10 EXERCISE: ANALYZE YOUR DIET

Diet Diary

Date	Time	Food Eaten	Estimated Portion	Estimated Calories	Activity

Next Steps

You now have all the information you need to explore your life and make healthy changes toward a new you. The last chapter will be the opportunity to review all we did throughout this whole book and start moving toward success.

TAP DANCE INSTRUCTION: CRAMP ROLL

The tap step that we are going to learn for chapter 10 is called the cramp roll. It is a fun and easy step to do. You start by digging the right ball of the toe into the floor, then the left, staying on your toes. You then drop the right heel followed by dropping the left heel. The timing is 1-2-3-4, or right, left, right left. You can do this step at any speed.

CHAPTER II:
ALIGNING ALL YOUR RHYTHMS

OBJECTIVES: CHAPTER 11

1. Review all that we have learned to this point

2. Marvel in your accomplishments

3. Start moving to your new life!

Congratulations! **You did it!** You have arrived at the last chapter. You may be feeling a little bit overwhelmed with all that you have learned. That is great. William Lee Raymond says that, "Within the depths of our being, there are secrets waiting to awaken." That is what you have done. You have awakened those secrets and have become aware of your reality. You have conducted several exercises in self-exploration and have increased you understanding of yourself. This understanding is what can increase your capacity for change. We won't ever change if we don't believe that there is a need to change or understand where and what to change. This book has been a systematic process to help you analyze your personal rhythms in your daily life so that you can identify what needs to change. What you have probably found is that some of your rhythms are good and some may not be good. Let's review all we've done through the chapters.

Chapter 1

Chapter one was all about rhythms. This chapter focused on the rhythms in the world, what they are and how we fit into the universe. You had the opportunity to find your basic rhythm patterns, see what they were like and how they may affect your life.

Chapter 2

Chapter two was all about rhythms and health. The intent of the information was to show you how personal rhythms can affect your health. The tool was designed to provide you with some insight into the status of your personal health. It also gives you some ideas of what you can do to improve your health so you can look forward to a healthy future.

Chapters 3, 4, and 5

Chapters three, four, and five were all about self-exploration, organization, and personal drive. These were the chapters on values, goals, and objectives. They began to answer the questions of who you are and why you are. Hopefully, the exercise you did on values helped you learn about the motivation behind your behaviors. You then learned to take those behaviors and identify goals for yourself that align with your values. Lastly, you developed your objectives to help you achieve your goals.

Chapter 6

In Chapter six, we went over the top and started talking about mental rhythms and positive thinking. Here we began to explore the mind and the contribution of our mental processes to healthy rhythms. The exercise for this chapter identified fear, your negative thought rhythms, and your strategies for flipping those negative thoughts to positive.

Chapter 7

Chapter seven focused on the rhythms of stress and how dangerous stress can be in our lives. The tool provided an opportunity for personal reflection into finding your fears and stressors and then how to control them.

Chapters 8, 9 and 10

Chapters eight, nine, and ten focused on the Trifecta of health and the identification of our personal rhythms of exercise, sleep, and nutrition. All three of these are vital to our health and to our personal success. Several tools throughout this chapter helped you identify ways to improve your rhythms in these areas.

Rhythm Success Factors

Here is what I call rhythm success factors to help you live healthier and happier and achieve your goals.

You Are Human!

First of all, realize that you are human. No matter how hard you try, you will continue to fall back to old rhythms. Just pick yourself up again and move on. That is okay! We're human. When you were learning to walk, you fell hundreds of times. You never gave up but pressed on with unrelenting perseverance. You can still rekindle that perseverance.

In my personal training days, I heard people say over and over when they blew their diet, "I will start tomorrow, or next week." I would always say, "Why waste that time? Restart your diet with your next meal." Don't give yourself license to wait!

Be Kind to Yourself!

Be kind to yourself. Don't beat yourself up. Love and forgive yourself and just move on. Remember, it is what it is. If you continue to focus on the negative, you will become stuck in that wasteland of negativity, which will always hold you back. You are an incredibly unique individual. No one else has the qualities that you do. Enjoy the fact that you are you!

Find a Support System

We have talked about this before, but it is so important that it bears repeating. Share your goals and desires with someone you love or respect and ask them to help you! Ask and you shall receive. We are not all good at that. It is incredibly difficult for me to ask for help. Maybe it comes from the fact that I was the oldest in my family, and the need for me was to be independent and responsible. Regardless of the reasons, just ask.

Review Your Goals and Objectives Regularly

Make your goals and objectives a living document that you review regularly, at least monthly, or better yet, weekly. This will keep your mind channeled on where you plan to go. Feel free to change your goals and objectives based on changes in your life. Nothing stays the same, and at times we need to change course. Also, share this document with all the important people in your life so they can help you.

Education

Probably the greatest gift to give yourself is education whether it is formal in a school or university, informal through exploration, research or reading. Education and learning opens your eyes in a whole different way and presents so much more of the world to you. Even if you think that certain topics or experiences are out of your reach, try it and do the research. Education can apply to your fitness goals, your career goals or for personal leisure and interest. For everything you want to do in your life, search for the education to help you.

Celebrate Your Success

Remember that celebration validates our success and says to the world that we have accomplished something wonderful. Take time to be proud of yourself. Don't be afraid to smile and to let others know that you feel good about what you have achieved, no matter how small you may think the accomplishment is.

Enjoy The Journey

Remember that your life goals are a journey that can be summed up in this chart, which is your personal roadmap to success. It begins with our first step of self-discovery and self-knowledge. The next step in the journey is finding your personal rhythms and then moving along your continuum to your ultimate life goals. Along the way we may need to find ways to become more positive and to control stress. Lastly, the Trifecta of health will keep our bodies strong and ready to meet any challenge life presents to us.

Nothing But Rhythms and Change

After all, life is nothing but rhythms, and rhythms can change. We are creatures of habit, but we are very good at change even though we are, at times, uncomfortable with change. Maybe you have been married, maybe you have gone to school, you have changed jobs, and you probably have moved. You bought new furniture, and you have bought cars. All of these examples represent your ability to change and to change successfully. The whole key to successful change is remaining in control of the change, which is achieved through good planning and well thought out life goals.

Dancing Through Life

Take a look around. We are all part of this huge, wonderful universal dance. Everybody is dancing following his or her own personal rhythms. To all of you who have taken the time to read this book, I just want to say congratulations and good luck on a successful journey. **Always remember that you can do this!**

GLOSSARY OF TAP TERMS

Ball change: Transfer of weight onto the toe of one foot, behind the other foot followed by transferring weight back to the front foot.

Bombershay: Traveling step to the side such as step, brush, toe step etc.

Brush: Hitting the floor with the ball of the foot in a forward movement.

Buffalo: Jump on one leg, shuffle opposite leg and jump back onto first leg.

Chug: Flat foot slide on one foot forward supporting total weight of the body.

Chug shuffle: Chug followed by a shuffle with the opposite foot.

Clap: Impact of two hands to create sound.

Click: Tapping the toes or the heels together on the ground or in the air.

Cramp roll: Four quick moves in sequence, toe, toe, heel.

Dig: Tapping of ball of the foot or heel forcefully into the floor.

Drop: Lowering heel of foot while on the ball of supporting leg.

Flap: Forward brush of the toe followed by placement of the foot on the floor to create two quick sounds.

Flea Hop: Slide to the side while moving hips R-L.

Heel: Dropping the heel to the floor usually combined with another move such as heel dig or heel drop.

Hop: Lifting off the floor and returning on the same foot.

Jump: Lifting off the floor and landing on the opposite foot.

Maxieford: Jump on one foot, shuffle the other, jump onto the foot shuffled and toe back with the opposite foot.

Nerve tap: Quick small repeated tapping of one toe into the ground.

Over the top: Jumping over the other leg.

Paddle: A series of heel drops performed between pulls in quick succession.

Paddle roll: Paddle followed by a ball-heel.

Pick up: Pull back of the toes accomplished by lifting and bending knees.

Pull: A brush back motion of the ball of the foot.

Riff: Brush and scuff forward of one foot ending in the air.

Riffle: Brush and scuff forward of one foot ending in the air followed by a brush back.

Riff drop: Brush and scuff forward of one foot ending in the air followed by a heel drop of the supporting foot.

Scuff: Forward brush of the heel ending in the air.

Scuffle: Forward brush of the heel ending in the air followed by a brush back.

Shuffle: Brush forward with the ball of the foot followed by a brush back.

Slap: Brush forward of the foot followed with the placement of the same foot on the floor yielding two quick sounds.

Spank: Forceful pull back of the toe.

Stamp: Full footstep in any direction changing weight.

Step: Flat foot transfer of weight from one foot to the other.

Stomp: Full footstep that does not transfer weight.

Tap: A step on the ball of the foot with or without a weight change.

Tap Walk: Deliberate separation of heel and toe drops in walking motion to create two sounds.

Time step: A four count movement alternating sides and changing weight.

Toe stands: Balancing on the tips of the toes of the tap shoes.

Trench: Jumping forward from one foot to another while brushing your legs to the back.

Waltz clogs: Step shuffle ball change alternating done in a waltz tempo.

Wings: Jump while scraping both legs to the sides while elevating.

REFERENCES

Blanchard, K. (Apr, 1997). You are your own best friend. *Executive Edge, 28(4), 4-5.*

Department of Agriculture. (2007). New Food Pyramid.

Frankl, V. E. (1998). *Man's Search for Ultimate Meaning* (1st ed.). New York: Knopf.

Georgescu, P. (2005). *The Source of Success: Five Enduring Priniples at the Heart of Real Leadership.* .Business Book Review 22(38).

Johnson, R. J. (July, 2005). Saying no to negativity. *Canadian Journal of Health and Nutrition, 273(2) 56-57.*

Godwin, J. (April, 2006). Should we be teaching values or virtues. *Primary and Middle Educator, 4(1).*

Griffith, B., Graham, C. (Spring, 2004). Meeting needs and making Meaning: The pursuit of goals. *Journal of Individual Psychology, 60(1), 25-41.*

Hinsz, V.B. (2004). Repeated success and failure influences on self-efficacy. *Social Behaviior and Personality, 32(2). 191-197.*

Jones, M.L. (Aug, 2006). What is your mission? *Journal of Financial Planning, 19(8), 42-43.*

Lippitt, G.L. (Oct, 1979). Learning Rhythms. *Training & Development Journal, 33(10) 12-21.*

Mason, Keith. (Dec, 1998). The power of thoughts over the physical body. *Positive Health, 35, 21-23.*

McGarver, A.R., Warner, R.M. (May, 2003). Attraction and Social Coordination: Mutual Entrainment of Vocal Activity Rhythms. *Journal of Psycholinguistic Research, 32(3), 335-354.*

Natenberg, T. (May, 2004). Define goals to achieve them. *Selling, 1-4.*

Nourie, D. (Sep, 2001). Your Internal Clock. *Children's Digest, 51(6), 10-11.*

Rusak, B., Zucker, I. (1975). Biological rhythms and animal behavior. *Department of Psychology, UofC.*

Smolensky, M, Lamberg, L. (2000). *The Body Clock: Guide to Better Health.* Henry Holt & Co.

Stepanek, M. (Jul, 2006). Goal Getters. *Personal Excellence, 11(7), 15.*

Suvobrata, M. Riley, M. (Sep, 1997). Chaos in human rhythmic movement. *Journal of Motor Behavior. 29(3), 195-199.*

Taymour, Qabazard. (Feb. 2005). You are what you believe. *Positive Health, 108, 16-18.*

Underwood, A. (2004). We've got rhythm. *Newsweek, 144(15), 46.*

Vaughan, S. (May, 2000). There's Power in Positive Thinking. *Cosmopolitan, 228(5), 88.*

Warren, T. (Feb, 2006). Four traits of a great leader. *Credit Union Magazine.*

Weinberg, H. (July, 2005). The happiness formula. *ETC: A Review of General Semantics, 62(3), 298-299.*

Wilton, N. (Jan/Feb, 2002). Positive Outlook. *Yoga Journal, 165(78), 6.*

Wright, K. (Feb, 2006). Times of our lives. *Scientific American, Special Edition 16(1), 26-33.*